# THE STORY OF THE INDIAN MUTINY

First published 1896
This edition published by Lector House in 2023

ISBN: 978-93-5800-740-4


Lector House LLP
Registered Office: H. No. 96, Block C, Tomar Colony,
Burari, Delhi – 110084, India
info@lectorhouse.com
www.lectorhouse.com

# THE STORY OF THE INDIAN MUTINY

ASCOTT ROBERT HOPE MONCRIEFF

2023

LECTOR HOUSE

LECTOR HOUSE LLP

INTERIOR OF WELL AT CAWNPORE.

**Interior of Well at Cawnpore.**

*Frontispiece*

# THE STORY OF THE INDIAN MUTINY

BY

ASCOTT R. HOPE

AUTHOR OF
"MEN OF THE BACKWOODS," "YOUNG TRAVELLERS' TALES," ETC.

*WITH MAPS AND ILLUSTRATIONS*

# PREFACE

The story of the great Indian Mutiny has often been told in whole or in part. In this book, while historical outlines are carefully preserved, it is attempted to throw into relief the more picturesque episodes, and to bring out illustrative incidents of personal adventure likely to attract young readers. With such a theme, if any reader will only suffer some needful gravity in the introduction, he may be promised a narrative of heroism and romance which the dullest treatment could hardly make unexciting.

A.R.H.

# CONTENTS


| Chapter | | Page |
|---|---|---|
| | PREFACE | vi |
| I. | INDIA: ITS PEOPLES AND RULERS | 1 |
| II. | THE OUTBREAK | 10 |
| III. | THE SPREAD OF INSURRECTION | 19 |
| IV. | THE CONFLAGRATION | 29 |
| V. | THE CITIES OF REFUGE | 37 |
| VI. | THE FALL OF DELHI | 55 |
| VII. | THE DEFENCE OF LUCKNOW | 67 |
| VIII. | LORD CLYDE'S CAMPAIGNS | 82 |
| IX. | THE EXTINCTION | 94 |
| | APPENDIX | 100 |

# THE STORY OF THE INDIAN MUTINY

## CHAPTER I

### INDIA: ITS PEOPLES AND RULERS

A troubled history has all along been that of the great tongue of land which, occupying the same position in Asia as Italy in Europe, is equal to half our continent, with a population growing towards three hundred millions. Far back into fabulous ages, we see it threatened by mythical or shadowy conquerors, Hercules, Semiramis, Sesostris, Cyrus; whelmed beneath inroads of nameless warriors from Central Asia; emerging first into historical distinctness with Alexander the Great's expedition to the valley of the Indus, from which came that familiar name given to dark-skinned races on both sides of the globe. Our era brought in new wars of spoil or of creed; Tartars, Arabs, Turcomans and Afghans in turn struggled among each other for its ancient wealth; and India knew little peace till it had passed under the dominion of a company of British merchants, who for a century held it by the sword as proudly as any martial conqueror.

This rich region having always invited conquest, its present population is seen to consist of different layers left by successive invasions. First, we have fragments of a pre-historic people, chiefly in the hill districts to which they were driven ages ago, whose very tribe-names, meaning *slaves* or *labourers*, sometimes tell how once they became subject to stronger neighbours; but behind them again there are traces of even older aborigines. Next, the open parts of the country are found over-run by a fair-skinned Aryan race, of the same stock as ourselves, whose pure descendants are the high-caste Brahmins and Rajpoots of our day, while a mixture of their blood with that of the older tribes has produced the mass of the Hindoo inhabitants. Over them lie patches of another quality of flesh and blood, deposited by the fresh streams of Moslem inroad, as in the case of our Saxons and Normans. But whereas with us, Briton, Saxon and Norman are so welded into one nation, unless in mountainous retreats, that most Englishmen hardly know what blood runs mingled in their veins, here a very imperfect fusion has taken place between varied peoples, held jealously aloof by pride of race, by superstition, by hatred of rival faiths, and still speaking many different languages, with the mongrel mixture called Hindostani as the main means of intercommunication. The peculiarity of the latest conquest, our own, is that the dominant strangers show small desire to settle for life in the country subject to them, yet we have added a new element in the half-caste or Eurasian strain, through which, also, and but slightly by other means, have we been able to affect the religious belief of this motley population.

Religion may be taken as the keynote of Indian life and history. While our ancestors were still dark-minded barbarians, their Aryan kinsmen, migrating to Hindostan, had developed a singular degree of culture, especially in religious thought. Before Greece or Rome became illustrious, the hymns of the Vedas bespeak lofty ideas of the unseen, and the Brahminical priesthood appear as philosophers, legislators and poets of no mean rank. The first historical notices of India show a high level, not only of material but of moral civilization, as well as a manly temper of warriors well able to defend the soil they had won.

This enervating climate, however, with its easy efforts for existence, has proved an influence of degeneracy, and most clearly so in the matter of belief. Good seed, which here sprang up so quickly, was always apt to wither under a too scorching sun, or to run to rank foliage rather than to fruit. Early Brahminism, itself a marked growth in thought, after a time began to be choked by the heathenism it had overshadowed. It sent out a new shoot in Buddhism, a faith of noble ideals, which to this day surpasses all others in the number of its adherents. This, in turn, became a jungle of sapless formulas, and after a thousand years died out on the land of its birth. Then grew up modern Hindooism, a union of Brahminical dreams of divinity and Buddhist love for humanity, interwoven with the aboriginal superstitions, the whole forming a tangled maze, where the great Hindoo trinity of Brahma the Creator, Vishnu the Preserver, and Siva the Destroyer, take Protean shapes as a pantheon of innumerable gods, amid which higher minds may turn upwards seeking one Almighty Spirit, but the vulgar crowd fix their attention rather on grotesque idols, base fetishes, symbols of fear and sensuality, fitly adored with degrading rites and barbarous observances. All efforts have hitherto little availed to clear this deeply-rooted wilderness of misbelief. Enlightened Hindoos, who see the errors of their religion, yet find it difficult to shake off the mental slavery of the "unchangeable East." Our missionaries have to deplore the little real success that attends their efforts. Beneath the sweltering sky of Hindostan, spiritual life remains a day-dream or a nightmare; reformers are ever silenced by fanatics; virtues are frittered down into foolish scruples; harmful customs cumber the ground, hindering the growth of progressive institutions.

The great encumbrance of Indian life is the system of caste, doubly fostered by religion and pride of race. Originally the conquering Aryans became divided into *Brahmins* or priests, *Rajpoots* or warriors, and *Vaisyas* or husbandmen, still distinguished as the "twice-born" castes, who wear the sacred thread, badge of this spiritual aristocracy; while under the common name of *Sudras* or serfs, were included all the despised aboriginal tribes. Then the mixed population, formed by amalgamation between the latter and the lower ranks of their masters, went on splitting up into other recognized castes, as the superior classes, who took a pride in keeping their stock pure, grew themselves divided among separate tribes or castes; and thus arose a complex segregation of society into countless bodies, cut off from each other by almost impassable barriers of rank and occupation. There are now thousands of these castes, marked out by descent, by calling, or by locality, the members of which cannot intermarry, may seldom eat together, and must not touch food cooked by an inferior; even the shadow of an outsider falling upon his meal might cause a high-caste Hindoo to throw it away and go fasting. Each trade is a separate caste, each order of servant; and the man who makes his master's bed would shrink from the touch of the sweeper who cleans out his bath-room. Yet caste does not always coincide with social position; a powerful prince may be born of a low caste, and the native officer who gives orders to a high-caste Brahmin in the ranks, must bow before him when his sacred character is to be enlisted for the services of a family festival.

The origin of this organized exclusion becomes illustrated by the conduct of our own countrymen in India, among whom any penniless subaltern is apt to display at the best a haughty tolerance for the high-titled descendants of native kings, while he holds aloof from Englishmen of inferior station, and openly despises the half-caste Eurasian, who in turn affects contempt for the heathen Hindoo. We, indeed, have common sense enough, or at least sense of humour, not to let our prejudices degenerate into the ridiculous scrupulosity which forbids a Rajah to dine in the same room with his guests, or a coolie to set profane lips to his neighbour's drinking vessel. Railway travelling, military service, association with Europeans, cannot but do much to break down these burdensome restrictions; and enlightened natives, in public or in private, begin to neglect them, though it is to be feared that they too often copy the worse rather than the better parts of our example. But among the mass of the ignorant people, the least infringement of the rules of caste is looked upon with horror, and to become an outcast *pariah*, through any offence against them, is the ruin in this world which it seems in the next.

Another main barrier to progress here, has long been the slavish condition of women, not improved by the next creed which came to modify Hindoo institutions. Buddhism was hardly extinct in India, when Mohamedan incursions began to put a strain of new blood into the physical degeneration of the Hindoos, and though the Crescent, except in parts, has never superseded the symbols of the older religion, these two, dwelling side by side, could not be without their reaction on each other's practice. It was the north of the peninsula that became most frequently overflowed by inroads of its Moslem neighbours, while Hindooism was left longer unassailed in the south, where also the aboriginal fetish worships had of old their citadels. Even in the north the conquests of Islam were long temporary and partial, irruptions of pirates or mountain-robbers, able to prey upon the wealth of India only through the want of cohesion among its Rajpoot lords. These early invaders either returned with their booty, or remained to quarrel over it between themselves, or were spoiled of it by fresh swarms from beyond the Himalayas.

By the beginning of the thirteenth century, we find a Mohamedan empire set up at Delhi by a dynasty known as the Slave Kings, who, before long, gave place to rival adventurers. The power of the Crescent now began to extend into Southern India, yet revolts of vassals and viceroys kept it continually unstable. At the close of next century, the redoubtable Tamerlane captured Delhi, giving it up to an orgy of slaughter; but this devastating conqueror retired beyond the mountains and left India divided between warring princes, Hindoo and Moslem. Four generations later, Tamerlane's descendant Baber returned to make more enduring conquests;

then it was by his grandson, Akbar, that the Mogul empire became firmly founded.

Akbar the Great, whose long reign roughly coincides with that of our Queen Elizabeth, was rarely enlightened for an Oriental despot. By a policy of religious toleration, he won over the Hindoo princes, while he reduced the independent Mohamedan chiefs under his authority, and did much towards welding Northern India into a powerful union of provinces, ruled through his lieutenants. His less wise heirs, cursed by self-indulgent luxury and by family discords, added to the splendour rather than to the strength of this dominion. Its last famous reign was that of Aurungzebe, covering the second half of the seventeenth century. A bigoted Mohamedan, he alienated the Hindoos by persecution, while he spent many years in conquering the independent Moslem kings of the south, only to ripen the decay of his vast empire. After his death, it began to go to pieces like that of Alexander the Great. His feeble successors dwindled into puppets in the hands of one or another artful minister. Their satraps at a distance, under various titles, asserted a practical autocracy. And now had sprung up a new Hindoo power, the warlike hordes of the Mahrattas, whose great leader Sivajee, from his hill-forts among the Western Ghauts, began to make these ravaging horsemen feared far and wide, till their raids were the terror of all India.

Among the quickly-fading glories of the Mogul Empire, almost unnoticed came the appearance of the new strangers who would inherit it. The Portuguese were the first Europeans to arrive, at the beginning of the sixteenth century, when all the gorgeous East was still a wonderland of wealth in Christian imaginations. Then followed the Dutch, who, however, fixed their chief attention upon the spice islands of the Archipelago. On the last day of A.D. 1600, the East India Company was incorporated by royal charter at London, none yet dreaming to what greatness it would rise. A few years later, an English ambassador, sent by James I., made his way to the Court of the Great Mogul, and received assurances of favour and encouragement for trade. About the same time, our first settlement was made on the Coromandel coast. In 1615 a factory was established at Surat, on the other side of India; then, half-a-century later, the head-quarters of the enterprise were shifted to Bombay, ceded by Portugal in 1661, which, being an island, seemed safe from Sivajee's plundering horsemen.

In the meanwhile, other trading stations had been acquired in Bengal. At the end of the century, the Company is found taking a more independent stand, purchasing land, erecting fortifications, and arming its servants to resist the dangers which threatened trade in this disordered region. Such was the humble origin of the three Presidencies of Madras, Bombay, and Bengal, the last of which became the most important, and its chief station, Calcutta, the residence of the Governor-General.

Other European nations appeared in the field, but our only formidable rival here was France, the Portuguese making little of their claim to monopoly, now represented by the settlements of Goa, best known as the breeding place for a mongrel race of servants. One more stock of emigrants must not be omitted from mention. Centuries before a European ship had touched India, a remnant of Persian fire-worshippers, flying from Mohamedan persecution, settled upon the west coast, where, though few in numbers, by their wealth, intelligence, and commercial enterprise, these Parsees have grown to be an influential element in the population, excelling, like the Jews in Europe, as traders and men of business.

The eighteenth century saw the ruin of Aurungzebe's empire going on apace. Sikhs and Rajpoots threw off its yoke; hereditary kingdoms were clutched for themselves out of the wreck by its ambitious viceroys; in 1739 the Persian Nadir Shah plundered the treasures of Delhi; after him came fresh hordes of Afghan horsemen. The greatest power in India was now the Mahratta Confederacy, under hereditary ministers bearing the title of Peshwa, who, like the Mayors of the Palace in Old France, usurped all real power, keeping Sivajee's unworthy heirs in sumptuous seclusion; a form of government that has often been brought about in Oriental States. The Peshwas, with their capital at Poona, ruled over the Deccan, the great tableland of the south; but the Mahratta incursions were carried as far as Delhi and Calcutta; and throughout India reigned a lawless disorder, inviting the interference of any hand strong enough to seize the opportunity.

It was the French who, having failed as traders, first sought to make political profit out of this confusion. Dupleix, Governor of Pondicherry, conceived lofty ideas of founding a new empire under the shadow of the old one, and to this end, began by trying to get rid of his English neighbours. In 1746 Madras was captured by the French, to be restored indeed at the peace of Aix-la-Chapelle; but though there came peace in Europe between the two nations, their East India Companies remained at jealous war. Dupleix, mixing in the intrigues of native ambition, made himself, for a time, predominant in the south; and we seemed like to lose all hold here, but for the appearance on the scene of one who was to prove arbiter of India's destinies.

Every one knows how the young subaltern Robert Clive, by his gallant defence of Arcot, suddenly sprang into fame, and at once turned the scale of prestige in favour of his countrymen. The French went on losing influence, till, in 1761, it was the turn of their settlements to be conquered. Dupleix died in disgrace with his ungrateful sovereign, while Clive was heaped with honours and rewards, soon earned by services in another field of action.

Before the French were fully humbled in the south, he had been summoned to Calcutta to chastise the despicable Nawab of Bengal, Surajah Dowlah, for that notorious atrocity of the "Black Hole," where nearly a hundred and fifty Englishmen were shut up in a stifling den not twenty feet square, from which few of them came out alive. Following Dupleix's example, Clive plunged into political intrigue, and undertook to supplant Surajah Dowlah by a prince of his own choosing. At Plassey, with three thousand men, only a third of them Europeans, he routed the tyrant's army, fifty thousand strong—a momentous battle that counts as the foundation of our sovereignty in India. A new Nawab was set up, nominally under appointment from Delhi, but really as the servant of the English Company, who now obtained a considerable grant of land as well as an enormous sum in compensation for their losses by Surajah Dowlah's occupation of Calcutta. A few years later their nominee was dethroned in favour of a more compliant one, who also had to pay handsomely for his elevation. He ventured to rebel, but to no purpose. Lord Clive pushed the

English arms as far as Allahabad; and henceforth, with whatever puppet on the throne and with whatever show of homage to the high-titled suzerain at Delhi, the Company were the actual masters of Bengal.

All over India spread the renown of Clive's small but well-trained Sepoy army. His subjugation of the effeminate Bengalees, Macaulay may well compare to a war of sheep and wolves; but this young English officer went on to defy the more warlike levies of the north-west. He seized the Dutch settlements that threatened armed rivalry in Bengal; he almost extinguished the French ones. A harder task he had in curbing the rapacity of his own countrymen, who, among the temptations that beset such rapid ascendancy, bid fair to become the worst oppressors of their virtual subjects.

The next great ruler of Bengal was Warren Hastings, who organized a system of administration for the territory conquered by Clive, and began with collecting the revenues directly through the hands of English officers. Private greed was now restrained; but the Governor must justify his policy and satisfy his employers, by sending home large sums of money, which in the long run had to be wrung from the unhappy natives; and this necessity led the agents of the Directors into many questionable acts. It was a great step from the fortified trading posts of last century to levying taxes and tribute, maintaining an army and navy, selling provinces and dictating to princes. But by this time the conscience of the English people was being roused, and it began to be understood how India, for all its princely treasures, was the home of a poor and much-enduring population, which our duty should be to protect rather than to spoil. Returning to England, Warren Hastings was solemnly impeached before the House of Lords for his high-handed oppression. That famous trial, in which more than one English Cicero denounced our pro-consul as a second Verres, dragged itself out for seven years, and ended in a verdict of acquittal, which posterity has not fully confirmed, yet with the recognition of extenuating circumstances in the novelty and difficulty of the criminal's office.

We now held the valley of the Ganges up to Benares, and were soon making further acquisitions in that direction. In the Bombay Presidency we came into collision with the Mahrattas, in Madras with Hyder Ali, the tyrant of Mysore. The result of these wars proved our arms not so invincible as in the case of the timid Bengalees, but more than one gallant action made native princes cautious how they trifled with our friendship. Fortunately for us, the mutual jealousy of neighbour potentates prevented them from combining to drive our small armies out of India, and we were able to deal with them one by one. We had now no European rival to fear, though more than one Indian despot kept French troops in his service, or natives trained and officered by Frenchmen. Napoleon Bonaparte, most illustrious of French adventurers, had an eye to romantic conquest in the East; but we know how he found occupation elsewhere, and did not come here to meet the adversary who in the end proved his master. For it was in India that Wellington won his first laurels, under his brother, Lord Wellesley, a Governor-General resolute to make England paramount over the ruins of the Mogul Empire. The Nizam of Hyderabad was persuaded to dismiss his French guards, and become the vassal of England, as his descendant still is. Tippoo, Hyder Ali's son, fell at the renowned storm of his stronghold, Seringapatam, in the last year of the century. The Mahrattas were attacked in the Deccan, where Wellington gained the battle of Assaye, while in the north Lord Lake mastered Delhi and Agra. But the princes of this great confederacy were not fully humbled till the third Mahratta war in 1818, under the Governorship of Lord Hastings; before which the Goorkhas of the Himalayas, and the Pindaree robbers of Central India, had also been taught the lesson of submission. Presently we were carrying our arms across the sea, and wresting Assam from the Burmese. The crowning exploit of this victorious period was the siege of Bhurtpore, a fortress believed in India to be impregnable, from which in 1805 an English army had fallen back, but now in 1827 its capture went far to make the natives look on us as irresistible. The once-dreaded name of the Emperor was a cloak for our power, as it had been for the Mahrattas', while Calcutta had taken the place of Delhi as capital, through the primacy of Bengal among the three Presidencies, whose bounds had stretched to touch each other all across India.

Lord William Bentinck, who now became Governor-General, earned a different kind of glory by his sympathetic labours for the true welfare of the millions whom those wide conquests had placed under our rule. He began to make war on the crimes of barbarous superstition—the burning of hapless widows, the murders of infants, the secret assassinations by fanatical devotees. But with his successor opened a new series of campaigns that were not always illustrious to the British arms. Russia had taken the place of France as the bugbear of our Indian predominancy. Alarmed by Muscovite intrigues in Afghanistan, Lord Auckland entered upon a course of unwise and disastrous interference with the politics of that country. We succeeded in dethroning the usurper, Dost Mahomed, of whom we could more easily have made an ally. But in 1841 the people of Cabul rose against us; our army of occupation had to retreat in the depth of winter; assailed by hardy mountain tribes, they perished miserably among the rocks of the Khyber Pass; and out of thousands only one man reached Jellalabad to tell the tale. Sale's brave defence of that poor fortress did something towards retrieving our disgrace, and next year an avenging army returned to work bootless destruction at Cabul, leaving a legacy of ill-will that has been dearly inherited by our own generation.

More substantial conquests followed. Scindia, one of the old Mahratta princes, was brought more effectively under British control. At the same time, the Moslem Ameers of Scinde were overcome by Sir Charles Napier. We then stood face to face with the last great independent power of Hindostan, and the foeman who proved most worthy of our steel. The Sikhs, a manly race, originally a sect of Hindoo reformers, had risen from Mogul persecution to become lords of the Punjaub, "country of the five rivers," which all along has been the great battle-field of Indian history. Runjeet Singh, their masterful ruler for forty years, had carefully avoided a struggle with the British, which soon after his death was brought on by the turbulent bellicosity of the people, made audacious through our Afghan reverses. The two Sikh wars of 1845 and 1848 were marked by long and desperate battles; Sobraon, Chillianwallah, and Goojerat are remembered for the bravery and the slaughter on both sides, but finally the Punjaub was over-run, disarmed, and turned into a British province.

Several smaller states also were annexed about this time, through the failure of legitimate heirs, and our Government's refusal to recognize the Hindoo custom of adoption. A second Burmese war resulted in the acquisition of another province beyond the Gulf of Bengal. Lastly, the King of Oudh, whose incapable tyranny seemed beyond cure, had to submit to be pensioned off and see his ill-governed dominions pass under British administration. This signalized the end of Lord Dalhousie's term of vigorous government, who, while carrying out a policy of somewhat high-handed annexation, had shown himself not less active in the construction of roads, canals, railways, telegraph lines, and in all ways accomplished much to extend, consolidate, and develop what, partly by accident, partly by force of circumstances, and partly by far-seeing design, had in less than a century become a mighty empire. There might well be elephants then alive that had served us when we were struggling to keep a precarious foothold on the coasts of India.

Such great and rapid changes could not be worked without leaving sore grudges and dangerous cankers of discontent. Our policy had been so much dictated by selfish strength, that it is no wonder if the natives should conceive respect rather than love for us. Even after higher motives began to come into play, our best intentions were apt to be misunderstood by those placed under us, or to be foiled by our own want of sympathy with and our ignorance of their feelings. The strong points and the weak ones of the two races are almost poles apart, and neither has proved ready to learn from the other. Our characteristic virtues of truth and honesty are hardly comprehensible to the slavish Oriental, who for his part displays a flattering courtesy and gentle kindliness, with which appears in harsh contrast our frankly blunt masterfulness, often degenerating into insolence of manner and foolish contempt for all that is not English. While many of our best officers have shown a spirit of enlightened and conscientious interest in their duties, the average Briton, who goes out to India merely to gain money more easily than at home, is unhappily too seldom the man to conciliate the prejudices of those whom he treats as contemptible "niggers," knowing and caring little about their ancient civilization. The very pride of our superiority seems against us: other conquerors, more willing to let themselves down to the level of the conquered, have proved less unsuccessful in winning their good-will. Still, these natives cannot but come to see the advantage of having rulers whose word may be trusted. For long, honest efforts have been made to exercise among all sects and classes an even-handed justice, hitherto little known in India, the chief hindrance to which lies in the corruption of the native subordinates, on whom our magistrates have largely to rely for the details of their administration.

At all events, the mass of the population, broken to the yoke of many masters, had accepted ours with apparent resignation, even if they might soon forget the grinding tyrannies from which we had delivered them. Some fiercer spirits muttered their hatred, but kept silence before our authorities. Some real grievances, here and there, passed too much unnoticed, and sufferings brought about by over-taxation or other injustice worked through the hasty inexperience of officials. In certain large towns, the suppressed rage of hostile believers was not always restrained from breaking into riot at the great religious festivals, but these outbreaks we could easily put a stop to; and the differences of creed and caste seemed our best security against any dangerous combination to expel us. Some princes, whose quasi-independent states were allowed to lie like islands among our fully-conquered territory, might at times uneasily remember the martial glories of their predecessors, but knew well how they held their idle sceptres only on our sufferance, and took care not to neglect any hint of good behaviour offered them by the British resident at their courts, as real an authority as the Peshwas or Nizams of the past.

From the Himalayas to Cape Comorin, from Beloochistan to the borders of China, England was recognized as the Paramount Power of this vast country, over which at length reigned the *Pax Britannica,* and seemed little like to be seriously disturbed when, in 1856, Lord Canning came out as Governor-General.

# CHAPTER II

## THE OUTBREAK

The almost complete conquest of India had been chiefly carried out through troops raised among its own natives, drilled and led by European officers. Here and there, in the course of a century, their commanders had been forced to repress attempts at mutiny, such as might take place in any army; but on the whole this Sepoy force had proved remarkably faithful to the Company in whose service haughty Rajpoot and warlike Moslem were proud to enlist, and counted for wealth its hire of a few pence a day. So great was the trust put in our native army, and so unexpected the outbreak of 1857, that we had then no more than about forty thousand English soldiers scattered over India, among six times their number of troops, who looked upon us chiefly as formidable masters.

Strict officers of the old school judged that the beginning of the mischief lay in making too much of our native soldiery. They had come to understand how far England's power in India depended upon them, while they were unable to form an adequate idea of its resources at the other side of the world. Changes in organization are accused of lessening the Sepoys' respect for their regimental officers, the best of whom, also, were commonly taken away from their military duties to fill coveted posts in the civil service. Flattery and indulgence had slackened their discipline at the same time that it came to be tried by unfamiliar causes of irritation. The main difficulty in managing these troops lay in the superstitious customs and prejudices which make so large part of a Hindoo's life. Our rule has been to respect their ideas of religion; but this was not possible in all the claims of military service. Sepoys believed their caste in danger, when called upon to cross the sea to make war in Burma or Persia. Marched into the cold heights of Afghanistan, they had to be forbidden the ceremonial daily bathings in which they would have devoutly persisted at the risk of their lives; and they fancied themselves defiled by the sheepskin-jackets given them there as protection against the climate. Through such novel experiences, suspicion began to spring up among them that the English designed to change their religion by force.

This suspicion grew to a height when, after the Crimean War, a wave of unrest and expectation passed over our Eastern possessions. In every bazaar, the discontented spoke ignorantly of the power of Russia as a match for their conqueror. Our disasters in Afghanistan had already shown us to be not invincible. An old story spread that the British rule was fated to come to an end one hundred years after the battle of Plassey, A.D. 1757. Now, the century having elapsed, secret messengers were found going from village to village bearing mysterious tokens in the shape of *chupatties*, flat cakes of unleavened bread, which everywhere stirred the people as a sacrament of disaffection. For once, Moslem and Hindoo seemed united in a vague hope that the time was at hand when they should be able to shake off the yoke of a race so repellent to both in faith, habits, and manners.

The centre of the agitation was in the north-western provinces of Bengal, where the recent annexation of Oudh, though meant as a real boon to the ill-governed people of that fertile country, had not been carried out without mistakes, wrongs and heart-burnings. Here also appeared a *Moulvie*, or prophet, like the Mahdi of the Soudan, preaching a holy war against the infidels, to excite the ever-smouldering embers of Mohamedan fanaticism, a revival of which has in our century spread all over the East. The Bengal army was mainly recruited from this region; and when the civil population were in such an unquiet state, we need not be surprised to find the Sepoys ripe for disorder, many of whom, deeply in debt to native usurers, had the natural desire of "new things," that, before and since the days of Cataline, has so often inspired conspiracies.

What brought their seditious mood to a head was the famous incident of the greased cartridges, often given as the main cause of the Mutiny, though it seems more justly compared to a spark falling upon an invisible train of explosive material. The Enfield rifle having been introduced into the native army, it was whispered from regiment to regiment that the new cartridges were to be greased with the fat of cows or of swine. Now, a chief point of Oriental religious sentiment is an exaggerated respect for animal life, carried so far that one sect of strict devotees may, in certain Indian cities, be seen wearing a cloth over their mouths, lest by accident they should swallow a fly; were they familiar with the discoveries of the microscope, they could only be consistent by abstaining from every drop of water. The cow is a special object of reverence among Hindoos, who are shocked by nothing so much as our apparent impiety in eating beef. The pig is held in detestation by Mussulmen. A majority of the Bengal army were high-caste Brahmins or Rajpoots, with an admixture of Mohamedans drawn from that part of India where their creed had taken firmest root. Both alike were horrified to think that they might be called on not only to handle but to touch with their lips such pollution as they imagined in animal fat.

It was in vain the Government proclaimed that no unclean matters should be used in the cartridges issued to them; that they might grease their cartridges for themselves; that they would be allowed to tear off the ends instead of biting them, as was the way in those muzzle-loading days. The suspicion had taken so strong a hold that in more than one case the new ammunition was mutinously rejected. Religious and political agitators eagerly seized this chance of fomenting their own designs. A fable spread among the Sepoys that the English, determined to destroy their caste as a preliminary to forced conversion, had ground up cows' bones to mix with the flour supplied to them. At Lucknow, the simple incident of a regimental surgeon tasting a bottle of medicine had been enough to raise a tumult among men who were convinced that he thus designed to pollute the faith of their sick comrades. Our officers, hardly able to treat such tales seriously, were forced to pay heed to the spirit underlying them, which through the early months of 1857 displayed itself ominously in frequent incendiary fires at the various stations, the stealthy Oriental's first symptom of lawlessness. Still, few Englishmen estimated aright the gravity of the situation; and the Government failed in the prompt severity judged needful only after the event. Two mutineers were hanged;[1] two insubordinate regiments had been disbanded, to spread their seditious murmurs all over Bengal; but the danger was not fully realized till, like a thunderbolt, came news of the open outbreak at Meerut, forty miles from Delhi.

The scenes of the Mutiny can ill be conceived without some description of an Indian "station." Usually the Cantonments lie two or three miles out of the native city, forming a town in themselves, the buildings widespread by the dusty *maidan* that serves as a parade-ground. On one side will be the barracks of the European troops, the scattered bungalows of officers and civilians, each in its roomy "compound," the church, the treasury, and other public places. On the other lie the "lines," long rows of huts in which the Sepoys live after their own fashion with their wives and families, overlooked only by their staff of native officers, who bear fine titles and perform important duties, but with whom the youngest English subaltern scorns familiar comradeship. Between are a maze of bazaars, forming an always open market, and the crowded abodes of the camp-followers who swarm about an Indian army.

At Meerut, one of the largest military stations in India, the native lines stretched for over three miles, and stood too far apart from the European quarters. Here were stationed more than a thousand English troops of all arms, and three Sepoy regiments, among whom the 3rd Light Cavalry had in April shown insubordination over the new cartridges. Of ninety men, all but five flatly refused to touch them when ordered. The eighty-five recalcitrants were arrested, tried by court-martial of their native officers, and sentenced to ten years' imprisonment. On Saturday, May 9th, at a general parade, these *sowars*, or Sepoy troopers, were put in irons and marched off to jail.

To all appearance, the mutinous feeling had been cowed by this example. But beneath the smooth surface, where English eyes had too little skill to read the native heart, were boiling fierce passions soon to take shape in reckless acts. Next evening, while our people were making ready for church, a disorderly band of sowars galloped to the jail, and released their comrades, along with many hundreds of other prisoners. Here was a ready-made mob of scoundrels, who at once began to plunder among the bungalows. The excitement quickly spread to the 11th and 20th native infantry regiments. Several of their officers hastened among them, trying to calm the tumult. But a cry arose that the European soldiers were upon them, and this drove the men of the 20th into a panic of fury. They stormed the "bells of arms," small dome-like buildings used as magazines, and got hold of their muskets. Colonel Finnis, commander of the 11th, had more success in quieting his men, but was shot down by the other regiment.

A murderous uproar broke loose through the Cantonments. The 11th are said

[1] Mungul Pandy was the first open mutineer executed at Barrackpore in April, from whose name, a common one among this class, the Sepoys came to be called "Pandies" throughout the war, a sobriquet like the "Tommy Atkins" of our soldiers.

to have refused to fire on their officers, and to have escorted white women and children out of danger; but their good dispositions were soon swept away in the torrent of disorder. The Sepoys of the 20th and 3rd Cavalry fell to shooting and hacking every defenceless European they met with. A crowd of *budmashes*, "roughs," as we should call them, poured out of the city to share the congenial work of robbery and bloodshed, in which they took the foremost part. The thatched roofs of bungalows were easily set on fire, that the inmates might be driven out to slaughter. In an hour all was wild riot; and the sun set upon a fearful scene of blazing houses, shrieking victims and frenzied butchers, strange horrors of that Sabbath evening, too often to be renewed within the next few weeks.

The English troops, already assembled for Church-parade, should at once have been marched to crush this sudden rising. But the General in command showed himself incompetent. There were delays and mistakes; and not till darkness had fallen was a force brought up, too late to be of any use beyond scaring the plunderers. By this time most of the Sepoys had hurried off towards Delhi, leaving the gleaning of murder and pillage to the rabble. Our soldiers fell back to their own quarters, where were gathered for defence the whole Christian community, many of whom, bereaved and destitute, after barely escaping with their lives, saw the sky glowing from the conflagration of their ruined houses, and might be thankful if they had not to shudder for the unknown fate of husband or child. Eager officers vainly begged the General to spare them some small force with which the mob of mutineers could have been pursued and dispersed; at least to let them gallop through the night to Delhi, and give warning there of what was at hand. The man unluckily charged with such responsibility did nothing of what might well have been done—a neglect which was nearly to cost us our Indian Empire.

To both sides, the securing of Delhi was of the highest importance. This magnificent city, in native eyes, still enjoyed the prestige of a capital. Its ancient renown and famous monuments made it specially sacred for the Mussulmen, whose rule had once flourished here. In its vast palace still lived the descendant of the Great Moguls, a feeble old man, who, under the shadowy title of king, was allowed, among thousands of poverty-stricken kinsmen and retainers, to retain in part the pomp, if not the power, of his haughty ancestors. To keep up the show of his sovereignty, the English refrained from occupying the city with their troops, who lay quartered outside, beyond a ridge overlooking it from the north; and even here there were no English soldiers. Such was the prize about to fall easily into the hands of the rebels.

Their secret messengers had already let the discontented within the city know what might be expected, while the only hint our officers had was in the breaking of the telegraph wire from Meerut. Still, uneasy vigilance being the order of the day, the authorities were on Monday morning startled by the report of a number of horsemen hurrying along the Meerut road. The magistrate, Mr. Hutchinson, at once galloped out to the Cantonments to warn the Brigadier in command, then returned to the city, where the chief civil officials had hastened to their posts, though hardly yet aware what danger was at hand. But, before anything could be done to stop them, the van of the mutineers had crossed the bridge of boats and seized the

Calcutta Gate, the guard of native police offering no resistance; and the way was thus clear for the main body following not far behind. A second band of troopers forded the Jumna, and entered the city at another point.

Some of these forerunners made straight for the palace, which should rather be described as a fortified citadel, forced their way into the presence of the doting old king, and, with or without his consent, proclaimed him leader of the movement. A swarm of his fanatical retainers eagerly joined them; they soon began to wreak their fury by massacring several Englishmen and ladies who had quarters here. Others broke open the prison and released its inmates, to swell the bloodthirsty mob gathering like vultures to a carcase. The main body of the mutineers, as soon as it arrived, split up into small bodies that spread themselves over the city for pillage, destruction and murder. In one quarter, there was a terrible slaughter of the poorer class of Europeans and of Eurasian Christians, who, in unusual numbers, lived within the walls of Delhi, not as elsewhere, under protection of the Cantonments outside. Women and children were ruthlessly butchered. Clerks, school-masters, printers, were killed at their work; doctors, missionaries, converts, none might be spared who bore the hated name. Some, flying or hiding for their lives, only prolonged their agony for hours or days. A few succeeded finally in making their escape. About fifty were confined miserably in an underground apartment of the palace, to be led out and massacred after a few days.

A regiment of Sepoys had been marched from the Cantonments to repress the disorder. But, as soon as they entered the city, they let their officers be shot down by the mutineers, and themselves dispersed in excited confusion. A detachment on guard at the Cashmere Gate held firm for a time, but evidently could not be depended on. Later in the day, they too turned upon their English officers. More than one officer was simply driven away by his men without injury; others were fired upon; others made their escape by leaping or letting themselves down into the ditch, as did several ladies who had taken refuge here with the main guard. These survivors fled to the Cantonments, where for hours their countrymen had been gathering together in almost helpless anxiety. No sure news came back from the city; but they could guess what was going on within from the uproar, the firing, the rising flames—at length from a sudden cloud of smoke and dust, followed by a terrible explosion, that marked the first heroic deed of the Indian Mutiny.

The magazine within the walls, on the site of the present post-office, was garrisoned by only nine Europeans under a young artillery lieutenant, named Willoughby. Set on his guard betimes, he took all possible measures for defence, calmly preparing to blow up the magazine, if it came to the worst. The native gunners soon deserted; the reinforcement urgently demanded did not appear; he found himself cut off in a city full of foes raging round his important charge, which presently, in the name of the King of Delhi, he was summoned to surrender. For a time this little band stood in trying suspense, while the insurgents worked up their courage for an attack. It appears that they expected the English troops to be upon them, hour by hour, and awaited the return of a messenger who could report the road from Meerut clear. Then on they came in crowds, storming at the gates, scaling the walls, to be again and again swept back by the fire of cannon in the hands of nine desperate men.

**Delhi, from the Outer Court of the Jumma Musjid.**

Three hours these nine held their post amid a rain of bullets, till Willoughby saw that he must be overwhelmed beneath numbers. One last look he took towards the Meerut road, in vain hope to see a cloud of dust marking the advance of the English troops that still lay idly there. Then he gave the word. In an instant the building was hurled into the air, with hundreds of its assailants, and it is said that five hundred people were killed in the streets by the far-reaching explosion. The man who had fired the train and two others fell victims of their courage; six managed to escape over the ruins in the confusion, poor Willoughby to be obscurely murdered two or three days later. The rest received the Victoria Cross, so often won, and still more often earned, in those stirring days. A son of one of these heroes is author of the well-known novel *Eight Days*, which, under a transparent veil of fiction, gives a minutely faithful description of what went on in and about Delhi at that terrible time.

Meanwhile, at the Cantonments, the officers' families and other fugitives had gathered in the Flagstaff Tower, a small circular building on the ridge, where, huddled stiflingly together, they suffered torments almost equal to those of the Black Hole of Calcutta. Their only sure guard consisted of the drummer boys, who, in Sepoy regiments, are usually half-caste Christians. These, armed for the nonce, were posted close round the tower; before it stood two guns served by native artillerymen to command the road from the city; and part of two regiments were still kept to a show of duty, but hourly their demeanour grew more threatening, till, when called upon to move forward, they at length flatly refused. Two or three gentlemen, stationed on the roof of the tower, in the scorching sun, held themselves ready to fire upon the first of their more than doubtful auxiliaries who should break into open mutiny. The Sepoys, for their part, under the eyes of the Sahibs, remained for a time in hesitation, uncertain how to act; and some of them allowed themselves to be deprived of their bayonets, which were stored away in the tower.

One messenger had ridden out towards Meerut to demand succour, but only to be shot down by the Sepoys. Another, disguised as a native, made the same attempt to no purpose. Brigadier Graves, still hoping for the arrival of European troops from Meerut, would not for a time hear of retreat. But when it became evident that the handful of band-boys and civilians were all he could trust to defend the tower packed with scared women and crying children; when fugitives from the city brought news that all there was lost; when the Sepoys here began to fire at their officers, whose orders were hardly listened to; when it became plain that the guns would not be used against the mutineers, he saw nothing for it but flight before darkness came on. Towards sunset, the refugees of the tower went off in disorder, on foot, on horseback, in their carriages, each as he could, many of the men hampered with helpless families. The Sepoys did not stop them; some even urged their officers to save themselves; but the guard of a large powder magazine refused to allow it to be blown up; and it proved impossible to carry off the guns.

Through the rapidly falling night, these poor English people scattered in search of safety, some making for Meerut, some northwards for Kurnaul, some wandering lost among the roused villages. Yesterday they had been the haughty lords of an obsequious race; now they were to find how little love had often been beneath the fear of English power. In many cases, indeed, the country-folk proved kind and helpful to bewildered fugitives; not a few owed their lives to the devotion of attached servants, or to the prudence if not the loyalty of native chiefs, who still thought best to stand so far on our side. But others, the news of their calamity spreading before them, fell into the hands of cruel and insolent foes, to be mocked, tortured and murdered.

Dr. Batson's adventures may be referred to, as one example of many. It was he, surgeon of a Sepoy regiment, who had volunteered, as above mentioned, to carry a message to Meerut in the disguise of a fakir, or religious beggar. Taking leave of his wife and daughters, he stained his face, hands, and feet to look like a native, and dressed himself in the costume which perhaps he had already used for some light-hearted masquerade. Thus arrayed, he made through the city without detection, but found the bridge of boats broken, houses burning everywhere, and country people rushing up to plunder the deserted bungalows. Turning back towards the Cantonments to reach a ferry in that direction, he excited the suspicion of some Sepoys, who fired at him; then he ran away to fall into the hands of villagers, who stripped him stark naked. In this plight, he had nothing for it but to hurry on after the fugitives making for Kurnaul. Before he had gone a mile, two sowars rode up to kill him. Luckily, Dr. Batson was familiar with the Mohamedan religion, as well as with their language; and while they ferociously cut at him with their swords, he threw himself on the ground in a supplicating attitude, praising the Prophet, and in his name begging for mercy, which was granted him as not seeming to be much of a Christian, or because they could not get at him without taking the trouble to dismount. Another mile he struggled on, then became surrounded by a mob, who tied the "Kaffir's" arms behind his back and were calling out for a sword to cut off his head, when some alarm scattered them, and he could once more take flight. His next encounter was with a party of Hindoo smiths employed at the Delhi Magazine. They stopped him, with very different intentions, for they invited the naked Sahib to their village, and gave him food, clothes, and a bed, on which he could not sleep after the strain of such a day.

For several days he remained in this village, the people taking a kindly interest in him on account of his acquaintance with their language and customs; and the fact of his being a doctor also told in his favour. But then came a rumour that all the Englishmen in India had been killed, and that the King of Delhi had proclaimed it death to conceal a Christian. On this, his native friends hid him in a mango grove, feeding him by night on bread and water. Nine days of anxious solitude he spent here, burned by the sun, scared at night by prowling jackals, but hardly thought himself better off when a new place of concealment was found in a stifling house out of which he dared not stir. It being reported that horsemen were hunting the villages for English refugees, his protectors thought well to get rid of him under charge of a real fakir, who carefully dressed and schooled him for the part. Through several villages they took their pilgrimage, and the disguised doctor passed off as a Cashmeeree fakir with such success that he got his share of what alms were going, and seems to have been only once suspected, through his blue eyes, by a brother holy man, who, however, winked at the deception. After wandering for twenty-five days, he had the fortune to fall in with a party of English troops.

Dr. Batson, we see, owed his escape to an intimate knowledge of the people, such as few Englishmen had to help them. His experience was that the Mohamedans were much more fierce against us than the mild Hindoo. But both religions had their proportion of covetous and cruel spirits, who at such a time would be sure to come to the front.

Like wolves scenting prey, gangs of robbers sprang up along the roads upon which the unfortunate travellers were struggling on, often under painful difficulties; and many fell victims whose fate was never rightly known. Others, wounded or exhausted, lay down to die by the way. Those who contrived to reach a haven of safety, had almost all moving tales to tell of adventure, of suffering, of perilous escape—tales such as, in the course of the next months, would be too common all over Northern India, and would not lose in the telling.

Many as these atrocities were, they might have been multiplied tenfold had the rebels acted with more prudence and less passion. So little did we know of the minds of our native soldiers, that it is still a matter of debate how far the Mutiny had been the work of deliberate design. But, at the time, it was widely believed by men too excited to be calm judges, that the outbreak at Meerut came a mercy in disguise, as it brought about the premature and incomplete explosion of a deep-laid plot for the whole Bengal army to rise on the same day, when thousands of Europeans, taken without warning and defence at a hundred different points, might have perished in a general massacre.

# CHAPTER III

## THE SPREAD OF INSURRECTION

"The Sepoys have come in from Meerut, and are burning everything.... We must shut up," had been the last message flashed from Delhi by a young clerk, who was killed in the act of sending it. This news, kept secret for a few hours by the authorities, was soon startling the English stations, north and west, and was put out of doubt by reports of the fugitives, as they came to spread their dismay from various points. On this side, fortunately, reigned the energy and foresight which had so disastrously failed at Meerut. Lahore, the capital of the Punjaub, swarmed with fierce fanatics, who would willingly have emulated the deeds of their brethren at Meerut and Delhi. In the Cantonments, a few miles off, were four regiments of Sepoys, held in check only by a small force of Europeans. But here Mr. Montgomery, the Commissioner in charge, showed a prompt mastery of the situation. He at once assembled a council of the chief civil and military officers; and, not without doubt on the part of some of his advisers, resolved to disarm the dangerous regiments before they should be excited to the revolt they were already conspiring.

Next day, May 12, a ball was to be given at the Cantonments. Lest the Sepoys should take warning, it went on as if nothing were the matter; but many of the dancers must have been in no festive mood, at a scene to recall that famous revelry on the night before Quatre Bras. The officers had their arms at hand in the ball-room. Dancing was kept up till two in the morning; then at early dawn, the whole brigade was turned out on the parade-ground. The native regiments were suddenly ordered to pile arms. They hesitated in obeying; but the thin line of English soldiers confronting them fell back to reveal twelve guns, loaded with grape, behind which the infantry ramrods rang fear into their doubtful hearts. Sullenly they gave up their arms, 2500 Sepoys cowed before not one-fourth their number. At the same time, the fort in the city was made safe by the disarming of its native garrison. Picquets of Europeans were posted at various points, and arrangements made for defence against any sudden rising.

Similar bold and prompt measures to secure other stations, forts, and arsenals of the Punjaub, at once checked the spread of the mutiny in this direction, and afforded a base of operations for its suppression. But, on other sides, it ran through the country like wild-fire—here blazing up into sudden revolt; there smouldering for weeks before it gathered head; at one place crackling out almost as soon as kindled; at another resolutely trampled down by vigilant authority; elsewhere quickly growing to a conflagration that swept over the richest provinces of India, unchaining the fiercest passions of its mixed population, and destroying for a time all landmarks of law and order. Men had to show, then, of what stuff they were made. While some of our countrymen gave way before the danger, or even precipitated it through panic or indecision, others stood fast at their posts, and by proud audacity were able to hold the wavering natives to allegiance, and still to keep hundreds of thousands overawed before the name of English rule. Not seldom was it seen how mere boldness proved the best policy in dealing with a race tamed by centuries of bondage; yet, in too many cases, gallantry, honour, devotion to duty, fell sacrificed under the rage of maddened rebels.

It is impossible here to track the irregular progress of the revolt, or to dwell on its countless episodes of heroism and suffering. Pitiable was the lot of all English people in the disturbed districts, most pitiable that of officials who, obliged to expose their own lives from hour to hour, had to fear for wife and child a fate worse than death. At their isolated posts, they heard daily rumours of fresh risings, treasons, massacres, and knew not how soon the same perils might burst upon themselves and their families. For weeks, sometimes, they had to wait in sickening suspense, a handful of whites among crowds of dusky faces, scowling on them more threateningly from day to day, with no guard but men who would be the first to turn their arms upon those whose safety was entrusted to them. To many it must have been a relief when the outbreak came, and they saw clearly how to deal with false friends and open foes. Then, at a season of the Indian year when activity and exposure are hurtful to the health of Europeans, for whom life, through that sweltering heat, seems made only tolerable by elaborate contrivances and the services of obsequious attendants, these sorely-tried people had to fight for their lives, pent-up in some improvised stronghold, wanting perhaps ammunition, or food, or, worst torment in such a climate, water, till relief came, often only in the form of death. Or, again, it might be their chance to fly, sun-scorched, destitute, desperate, skulking like thieves and beggars among a population risen in arms against the power and the creed they represented. It should never be forgotten how certain natives, indeed, showed kindness and pity towards their fallen masters. We have seen that in some cases the mutinous Sepoys let their officers go unhurt; occasionally they risked their own lives to protect English women and children against the fury of their comrades. But one horrible atrocity after another warned the masterful race how little they had now to hope from the love or fear of those from whom they had exacted such flattering servility in quiet times.

Among the natives themselves, the excesses of the Mutiny were hardly less calamitous. Many, if not most, were hurried into it by panic or excitement, or the persuasion of the more designing, and their hearts soon misgave them when they saw the fruit of their wild deeds, still more when they considered the punishment likely to follow. Anarchy, as usual, sprang up behind rebellion. Debtors fell upon their creditors; neighbours fought with neighbours; old feuds were revived; fanaticism and crime ran rampant over the ruins of British justice. Towns were sacked, jails broken open, treasuries plundered. Broken bands of Sepoys and released convicts roamed about the country, murdering and pillaging unchecked. Tribes of hereditary robbers eagerly returned to their old ways, now that our police need no longer be feared. The native police, themselves recruited from the dangerous classes, were frequently the first to set an example of rebellion. Not a few native officials, it should be said, gave honourable proofs of their fidelity, through all risks, while the mass of them behaved like hirelings, or displayed their inward hostility.

The more thoughtful part of the population might well hesitate on which side to declare; some prudently did their best to stand well with both, in case of any event; but those who had much to lose must soon have regretted the firm rule of our Government. On the whole, it may be said that the princes and nobles, where not carried away by ambition or religious zeal, remained more or less loyal to our cause, having better means than the ignorant mob of judging that our power would yet right itself, though crippled by such a sudden storm and staggering like to founder in so troubled waters. But in Oudh and other recently-annexed districts, where the Zemindars and Talookdars, or chief landowners, had often been treated with real harshness in the settlement of revenue, this class naturally proved hostile, yet not more so than the poor peasants, to whom our rule had rather been a benefit. The latter, indeed, acted in great part less like determined rebels than like foolish school-boys, who, finding themselves all at once rid of a strict pedagogue, had seized the opportunity for a holiday-spell of disorder; as with the Sepoys themselves, defection sometimes seemed a matter of childish impulse, and there would come a moment of infectious excitement, in which the least breath of chance turned them into staunch friends or ruthless foes. Except in Oudh, it may be said, the movement was in general a military mutiny rather than a popular insurrection, while everywhere, of course, the bad characters of the locality took so favourable an occasion for violence.

To gain some clear idea of what was going on over a region that would make a large country in Europe, it seems best to take one narrative as a good example of many. This means somewhat neglecting the rules of proportion required in a regular historical narrative. It will also lead to an overlapping of chapters in the order of time. In any case it must be difficult to arrange orderly the multifarious and entangled episodes of this story; and the plan of our book rather is to present its characteristic outlines in scenes which cannot always be shifted to mark the exact succession of events, but which will roughly exhibit the main stages of the struggle.

Let us, then, dismount from the high horse of history, to follow a representative tale of *Personal Adventures* by Mr. W. Edwards, Magistrate and Collector at Budaon in Rohilcund, the district lying on the Ganges between Delhi and Oudh. Almost at once after the outbreak at Meerut, his country began to show signs of epidemic lawlessness. Just in time, Mr. Edwards sent his wife and child off to the hill-station of Nainee Tal; then it was ten weeks before he could hear of their safety. A British officer, of course, had nothing for it but to stick to his post, all the more closely now that it was one of danger. The danger soon began to be apparent. What news did reach him was of robbers springing up all round, Sepoys in mutiny, convicts being let loose; and amid this growing disorder, he stood the ruler of more than a million men, with no force to back him but doubtfully loyal natives, and no European officials nearer than Bareilly, the head-quarters of the district, thirty miles off. His best friend was a Sikh servant named Wuzeer Singh, a native Christian, who was to show rare fidelity throughout the most trying circumstances.

At the end of the month, he had the satisfaction of a visit from one of his colleagues, and good news of a small Sepoy force, under an English officer, on its way to help him. But this gleam of hope was soon extinguished. For the last time, on Sunday, May 31st, he assembled at his house a little congregation with whom he was accustomed to hold Christian services. In the middle of the night, a sowar came galloping as for his life, to report that Bareilly was up, that the Sepoys there were in full mutiny, and the roads covered by thousands of scoundrels released from the jail. His brother magistrate at once dashed off to his own post. Mr. Edwards thought it his duty to remain to the last, like the captain of a sinking ship.

In the forenoon a few white men and Eurasians gathered at his house for poor protection. He wished them to disperse, believing that each could better escape separately, while their sticking together would only attract attention; but the others seemed too much overcome by fear to act for themselves, and refused to leave him. The stifling day wore on in anxious rumours. In the afternoon, the native officer in charge of the treasury came to ask Edwards to join the guard there, assuring him with solemn oaths that the men meant to be faithful. He was about to start, when Wuzeer Singh earnestly entreated him not to trust them. He took the advice, and afterwards learned that these men had been waiting to murder him. They would not come to his house, for fear the plundering of the treasury might begin in their absence.

About 6 p.m. the mutineers from Bareilly arrived; and tumultuous shouts announced that Sepoys, police, prisoners and all had broken loose at Budaon. Now the magistrate might think of himself, all show of authority being gone. He mounted his wife's horse, that had been standing saddled all day, and rode off, accompanied by two European indigo-planters and a Customs officer. His Eurasian clerk and his family he was obliged to leave, as they had no means of conveyance but a buggy, and the roads were blocked. All he could do for them was to consign them to the care of an influential native who happened to come up; and, as luckily these people were almost as dark as Hindoos, they succeeded in hiding themselves, at all events for a time.

Mr. Edwards had not ridden far when he met a Mohamedan sheikh, who proposed to him to take refuge at his house, some three miles in another direction. He turned with this well-wisher; then, passing his own bungalow again, saw how in ten minutes the plundering of it had already begun, his servants being first at the work. Wuzeer Singh and another faithful follower accompanied him, carrying 150 rupees in their waist-bands; that was all he had in the world but his watch, revolver, a little Testament, and a purse which had just arrived from England as a birthday present, which he kept about him as a dear gift rather than for use. Such a man in the East is not used to carrying money, but trusts his servants to act as purse-bearers, who will not cheat him more than is the custom. A groom had been entrusted with a change of clothes; but he soon disappeared.

When the party reached the house where they had been promised shelter, one of the family came out, respectfully informing their leader that they would not be safe here, but they must go on to a village about eighteen miles off. Mr. Edwards was much annoyed at this inhospitable reception, which afterwards turned out a blessing in disguise, for presently a band of horsemen arrived in search of him, and he would probably have been murdered, if he had not now been on the way to that further refuge.

Till midnight the fugitives rode through by-ways and fields, and villages swarming with armed crowds, who let the Englishmen pass in silence under the convoy of their chief. He took them to a house of his in a small village, where, after thanking heaven for their escape, they lay down to rest on the flat roof. The magistrate, for one, weary and worn out as he was, could hardly close an eye after the excitement of such a day. Early in the morning, they were roused up by the sheikh, who told them they must cross the Ganges at once, as their enemies would soon be in pursuit. So they did, fired at by an excited crowd assembled for the plunder of a neighbouring village, whose bullets luckily did not come near them.

On the other side, they were received by a Mohamedan gentleman, who was the more civil to them, as he heard that two English officials, with a large body of horse, were in the neighbourhood to restore order. Edwards and his party joined their countrymen, but found that the main body of expected troops had mutinied and made for Delhi, while their escort of sixty sowars was in such a doubtful disposition, that they were glad to send most of them off on pretence of guarding a treasury, which these men at once plundered, and dispersed.

With twenty troopers, whose fidelity they had to trust, the Englishmen started for Agra, but soon turned back, the road being blocked by mutineers marching to Delhi. They hardly knew which way to take. A party of two hundred Sepoys was reported to be hunting them out. Their escort grew so insolent, that they thought best to dismiss these fellows to go where they pleased; then, for a moment, it seemed as if the troopers were about to fall on them, but after a short consultation turned and rode off. The Englishmen, having been twenty hours on horseback, came back to the village from which they had started.

But they could not be safe here, and after a day's halt determined to separate. The other two civilians made a fresh attempt to push on for Agra. Edwards would not desert his companions, encumbrance as they were to him, for local chiefs, who might be willing to shelter Government officers at some risk, in the hope of getting credit for it on the re-establishment of our power, were unwilling to extend their services to these private persons. He had received a message asking him to come back to Budaon, as the mutineers had left it, and things were comparatively quiet there. He afterwards understood this to be a snare, the Sepoys being much exasperated against him because less money had been found in the treasury than they expected. But now he decided to return with the three who shared his fortunes.

They had first to cross the Ganges. On regaining the house of a zemindar, who had been a friendly enough host two days before, they met with a colder reception, for meanwhile this native gentleman had heard the worst news of the spread of mutiny. He agreed to provide them with a boat, but it proved too small to carry their horses across. All they could get out of the zemindar was an evident desire to be rid of them, and he strongly recommended them to make for Furruckabad, sixty miles off, where, he said, no mutiny had taken place. Hearing that the other side of the Ganges was all ablaze with pillage and destruction, they saw nothing for it but to follow this advice.

They set out, then, by night, and passed by several villages without being molested. At daybreak they reached a large place, where they presented themselves to the chief proprietor, who was polite, but would hardly let them into his house, while a brother of his, drunk with opium, seemed disposed to shoot them on the spot. The chief did relax so far as to give them some breakfast, then packed them off under escort of five horsemen to the care of a neighbour. Before leaving, he insisted on having a certificate that he had treated them well, a suspicious sign; and Wuzeer Singh overheard the escort saying that they were all to be killed. Putting a good face on the chance of having to fight for their lives, they reached a river-side village, where they were promised a boat to take them to Futtehgurh, the English station near Furruckabad. But instead of a boat, about the house in which they waited for it, a crowd of armed men appeared, with such menacing looks, that the Englishmen mounted and rode off, to find their way barred by a body of horse. They turned back. Then the crowd began to fire, and their escort at once galloped away. So did the Englishmen; but one of them, who rode a camel, fell into the hands of the mob and was cut to pieces.

The other three cleared a way for themselves, and rejoined their escort, who looked rather ill-pleased that they had escaped. Their leader, however, had shown some traces of pity, and now on Edwards appealing to him as a husband and a father, he undertook to save their lives if he could, and conducted them back to his master, who seemed sorry for what had happened, but would not keep them in the house beyond nightfall.

Disguised in native dress, their own clothes being burned to conceal all trace of their visit, they set forth again under the charge of two guides, and this time were more fortunate. Riding all night, once chased for their lives, at daybreak they reached the house of Mr. Probyn, Collector of Furruckabad, from whom they had a hearty welcome, but little cheering news.

The Sepoys at Futtehgurh had broken out, then had been brought back to their duty for a time, but could not be depended on. A large number of the Europeans had gone down the Ganges in boats to Cawnpore; others, among them Probyn's wife and children, were sheltered in a fort across the river, belonging to a zemindar named Hurdeo Buksh. Edwards was for going to Cawnpore, but that very day came the news of the rising there. After consultation with the officers at Futtehgurh, he agreed to accompany Probyn to Hurdeo Buksh's fort, where he found a number of acquaintances and colleagues living in great discomfort, and without much show of protection, in the dilapidated defences of this native stronghold.

Uncertainty and doubt reigned among these unfortunate people also. As the colonel of the Sepoy regiment at the station persisted in believing it staunch, and as some hopeful news from Delhi seemed calculated to keep it so, after two or three days most of the refugees returned to Futtehgurh. Probyn, however, preferred to trust his native friend; and Edwards, though the others judged him rash, decided to stay with Hurdeo Buksh. Here he was now joined by the faithful Wuzeer Singh, who had been separated from him in that riot on the river bank, but had lost no time in seeking his master out with the money entrusted to him.

When two days more had passed, a band of mutineers arrived from another station, flushed with massacre, and this was the signal for the Futtehgurh regiment to rise. The Europeans had taken refuge in the fort there; outside its walls all was uproar, villagers and Sepoys fighting for the plunder. Hurdeo Buksh at once assembled his feudal retainers, a thousand in number, and dug out from various hiding places the guns which he had concealed on the English Government ordering these petty chiefs to give up all their ordnance. He explained to his guests that a body of mutineers was coming to attack the fort, led by a false report that the two Collectors had several lakhs of treasure with them. They must at once go into hiding in an out-of-the-way village, as he could not trust his followers to fight for them. The Englishmen were unwilling to leave even such doubtful shelter as the fort offered, but when this Rajpoot chief gave them his right hand, pledging his honour for their safety, as far as in him lay, they knew he might be trusted, and consented to go.

Carrying their bedding, arms, and the Probyns' four little children, they crossed the Ramgunga, and reached the place where their quarters were to be, a filthy enclosure from which the cattle and goats were cleared out to make room for them. There at least they remained undisturbed; but after a few days were startled by sounds of heavy firing from Futtehgurh, where the Europeans were now being besieged in the fort. Contradictory rumours kept Probyn and Edwards in painful suspense, and when trustworthy news did come it was not assuring. The little force in the fort, some thirty fighting men, with twice that tale of women and children, could not hold out much longer. But several days and nights passed, and still the cannonading went on incessantly.

On the morning of the fifth day there was a sudden silence, which might mean that the attack had been given up, or that the resistance had been overpowered. Some hours later came fresh sounds of quick and irregular firing from another quarter, further down the river. While our miserable refugees were asking themselves what this portended, a messenger from Hurdeo Buksh came to tell them that the English had during the night evacuated the fort and fled in boats, only to be discovered and pursued, so the shots they now heard must be the death-knells of their wretched countrymen. Still, however, came conflicting stories. At one time the boats were said to be out of range, then to have sunk. The firing ceased, to break out again for an hour towards evening. At last they heard that one boat had escaped to Cawnpore, but that another had grounded, most of the people on board being massacred or drowned.

It would take too long to trace all the further perils of Edwards and the Probyns, who for weeks to come remained hidden in a cow-house for the most part, owing their safety chiefly to the heavy rains, that after a time turned their place of refuge into an island. Their presence here had been betrayed, and the

Nawab of Furruckabad kept pressing Hurdeo Buksh to give them up; but on the whole he proved a staunch protector, though more than once he seemed ready to get rid of so compromising guests. At one time, he had started them off by boat for Cawnpore, to certain death, as they believed; at another, they were to fly to Lucknow, disguised as natives, but that plan was frustrated by bad news of how things were going there; then again there was a design of smuggling them off to the hills; and once it was even proposed that they should abandon the children and take to the jungle. They were glad to be allowed to remain in their wretched shelter, where sometimes they durst not show themselves, or the rain kept them close prisoners. Poor Mrs. Probyn's baby wasted away for want of proper nourishment. When it died they had to bury it in the darkness, thankful to find a dry spot on which to dig a grave. Another of the children had the same miserable fate. The whole party grew thin and weak on their poor native fare. Two books they had, which were a great comfort to them, a Bible and a copy of *Brydges on Psalm cix.* On the fly-leaf of the latter Edwards wrote a note to his wife at Nainee Tal, and had the joy of hearing from her that she and his child were safe. The natives who carried these communications did so at the risk of their lives; but the severity used to any one caught acting as messenger for the English, did not prevent more than one letter from reaching the refugees.

Their native neighbours, on the whole, were kind, at least not showing any hatred towards them. By and by both Hurdeo Buksh and his dependents began to exhibit more active friendship, a sign of the advance of the English troops to reconquer the districts deluged by rebellion. Finally, at the end of August, their miserable condition was relieved by a message from General Havelock, who had now reached Cawnpore. Thither they set out, running the gauntlet of fresh dangers on the river, and could hardly believe their good fortune when at length they found themselves safe among British bayonets. The whole story is a most moving one, and should be read in full in Mr. Edwards' book, to the interest of which this abridgment by no means does justice, since its object is rather to show the state of the country than to enlarge on individual adventures and sufferings.

One passage in his party's obscure experiences brings us back to the highway of history. More than a month after the fall of Futtehguhr, there had appeared at their refuge a tall, lean, spectral-looking figure, almost naked and dripping with water, in whom Edwards with difficulty recognized a young Mr. Jones, heard of by them as having escaped from the boats to another of Hurdeo Buksh's villages. There he had been hiding ever since, and now, in his weak state, burst into tears at the sight of a countryman again and the sound of an English voice. From him they learned with horror all the particulars of the massacre that had been enacted within their hearing.

The little garrison of the Futtehgurh citadel had defended themselves till their ammunition was almost exhausted as well as their strength, while the Sepoys had begun to blow down their walls by the explosion of mines. Hampered by women and children, their only way of escape was the Ganges, that flowed by this fort. Early in the morning of July 3 they embarked in three boats to drop down the river. But their flight was soon discovered, and daylight showed them pursued by the bloodthirsty Sepoys. The swift current of the Ganges helped them so well that they might have got off safe but for the shallows that obstruct its channel. One of the boats soon grounded, and its people had to be transferred to another under fire. This second boat in turn, on which Jones now was, stuck fast on another sandbank opposite a village, the inhabitants of which turned out against it with matchlocks; and two guns opened fire from the bank. As the men were repelling this attack, and trying in vain to move off their heavy ark, there drifted down upon them a boat full of Sepoys, who, after pouring in a deadly volley, boarded the helpless craft. Most of its passengers, not already killed or wounded, jumped overboard. What followed, as related by Jones to Edwards, makes a too true picture of that terrible time.

"The water was up to their waists, and the current running very strong; the bottom was shifting sand, which made it most difficult to maintain a footing, and several of those who took to the river were at once swept off and drowned. Jones himself had scarcely got into the water when he was hit by a musket ball, which grazed the right shoulder, without damaging the bone. At the same moment he saw Major Robertson, who was standing in the stream supporting his wife with one arm and carrying his little child in the other, wounded by a musket ball in the thigh. Mrs. Robertson was washed out of her husband's grasp and immediately drowned. Robertson then put the child on his shoulder and swam away down the stream. Jones, finding that he could do no more good, wounded as he was, determined to try to save his own life by swimming down the river, hoping to reach the leading boat. As he struck out from the boat, he saw poor Mr. Fisher, the chaplain, almost in the same position as Robertson, holding his little son, a beautiful boy eight or nine years old, in one arm, while with the other he supported his wife. Mrs. Fisher was swaying about in the stream almost insensible, and her husband could with great difficulty retain his footing.

"When Jones had got clear of the boat, he continued alternately swimming and floating for five or six miles, when just as it was growing dusk, he saw the leading boat anchored for the night. He reached it, much exhausted by swimming, and by the pain of his wound and of his back; which, as he was naked to the waist, had been blistered and made raw by the scorching sun. On being taken on board, he found that the only casualty which had occurred to this party since leaving Futtehguhr, was the death of one of the Miss Goldies, who had been killed by a grape shot from one of the guns on the bank near Singheerampore.

"Mrs. Lowis—who had maintained her fortitude throughout, and was indefatigable during the siege in preparing tea and refreshment for the men—immediately got him some brandy and water and food, and he was then able to acquaint them with the miserable fate of his own party, of whom he supposed himself to be the sole survivor. The boat remained anchored in the same spot all night. Towards morning a voice was heard from the bank, hailing the boat. It proved to be that of Mr. Fisher, who, though badly wounded in the thigh, had managed by swimming a portion of the way, then landing and walking along the bank, to overtake the boat. He was helped on board more dead than alive, and raved about his poor wife and son, both of whom were drowned.

"At dawn they weighed anchor and proceeded down the stream; but very slowly, as there was no pilot or skilful steersman on board, and only the exhausted officers as rowers. Towards evening they became so exhausted that they made for a village on the Oudh side of the Ganges, in hopes of being able to procure some milk for the children and food for themselves. The villagers brought supplies, and did not show any ill-will or attempt to attack the party.

"The boat was so crowded with its freight of from seventy to eighty human beings, that Jones could find no space to lie down and sleep; he therefore determined, as he was quite exhausted, to go on shore and endeavour to get some rest. A villager brought him a charpoy, on which he lay down and fell fast asleep. He was roused by a summons from Colonel Smith to rejoin the boat, as they were on the point of starting; but finding himself very stiff and scarcely able to move, he determined to remain where he was, as he thought he might as well die on shore as in the boat: in either case he regarded death as inevitable. He therefore sent back a message that he could not come, and begged to be left behind. Colonel Smith after this sent him two more urgent requests to join the boat, which at length departed without him. He slept till morning, when a poor Brahmin took pity on him and permitted him to remain in a little shed, where he was partially sheltered from the sun. There he remained unmolested by the villagers, and protected by the Brahmin, until he was permitted to join us."

In the absence of other surgery, Jones had a happy thought for treating his wound, which else might have killed him by mortification. He got a little puppy to lick it morning and evening, then it at once began to improve. But he was still in a sorry state when, wading and swimming all night over the inundated country, he managed to join Edwards' party.

Two of his companions, who had also escaped alive, were hidden in other villages without being able to communicate with each other. Three unhappy ladies and a child had been taken back captive to Futtehguhr. There, three weeks later, by order of the Nawab, who played the tyrant here for a time, they were blown away from guns or shot down by grape, along with some scores of native Christians, on whom the Sepoys thus wreaked the infuriation of their defeat by Havelock's troops. The first boat's crew had gained Cawnpore, only to be involved in its still more awful tragedy.

Before coming to that part of the story, let us turn from the provinces now deluged by rebellion, to see what was being done elsewhere to make head against such a torrent.

# CHAPTER IV

## THE CONFLAGRATION

On the second day after the rising at Meerut, Calcutta had been electrified by a telegram from Agra. The central government seemed at first hardly to realize the gravity of the crisis. But when further bad news came in, Lord Canning recognized that our Indian Empire was at stake, and began to act with an energy, in which his character and his inexperience of Indian affairs had made him hitherto wanting; and if to some he seemed still deficient in grasp of such perilous affairs, it may be said of him that he never lost his head, as did others whose counsels were more vehement. He looked around for every European soldier within reach; he called for aid on Madras and Ceylon; he ordered the troops returning from the war happily ended in Persia, to be sent at once to Calcutta; he took upon himself the responsibility of arresting an expedition on its way from England to make war in China, but now more urgently needed for the rescue of India. Weeks must pass, however, before he could assemble a force fit to cope with the mutiny, while every English bayonet was demanded at a dozen points nearer the capital, and the Government knew not how far to trust its embarrassing native army.

All was confusion, suspicion, and doubt, when the first measures of precaution suggested by the danger might prove the very means of inflaming it. The practical question, anxiously debated in so many cases, was whether or no to disarm the Sepoys, at the risk of hurrying other detachments into mutiny, and imperilling the lives of English people, helpless in their hands. Most officers of Sepoy regiments, indeed, refused to believe that their own men could be untrue, and indignantly protested against their being disarmed—a blind confidence often repaid by death at the hands of these very men, when their turn came to break loose from the bonds of discipline. But one treacherous tragedy after another decided the doubt, sometimes too late; and where it was still thought well to accept the Sepoys' professions of loyalty, they were vigilantly guarded by English soldiers, who thus could not be spared to march against the open mutineers.

Paralyzed by want of trustworthy troops, Lord Canning could do little at present but give his lieutenants in the North-West leave to act as they thought best—leave which they were fain in any case to take, the rebellion soon cutting them off from communication with the seat of Government. But there, most fortunately, were found men fit to deal with the emergency, and to create resources in what to some might have seemed a hopeless situation. At the season when the Mutiny broke out, English officials who can leave their posts willingly take refuge at the cool hill-stations of the Himalayas. General Anson, the Commander-in-Chief, had betaken himself to Simla, the principal of these sanatoriums, lying north of Delhi and of the military station at Umballa. Here the alarming news came to cut short his holiday. Naturally reluctant to believe the worst, he yet could not but order a concentration of troops at Umballa, where he arrived in the course of three or four days.

A more masterful spirit was already at work upon the scene of action, if not by his personal presence, through the zealous colleagues inspired by his teaching and example as a ruler of men. Sir John Lawrence, Chief Commissioner of the Punjaub, had also been recalled on his way to the hills, to find himself practically independent governor of that side of India. At once rising to the emergency, as soon as he had taken the first measures, already anticipated indeed by his deputies, for the safety of his own province, he saw that the one thing to be aimed at was the recovery of Delhi, the very name of which would be a tower of strength to the mutineers. The Commander-in-Chief's eyes were mainly open to the difficulties of such an enterprise; and the staff, fettered by red-tape, cried out upon the impossibility of advancing in the unprepared state of his army. Lawrence never ceased to urge that, with or without guns and stores, everything must be risked to strike an immediate blow at Delhi, which might check the spread of rebellion by restoring our lost prestige. His tireless subordinates did the impossible in collecting supplies and means of transport. Anson, urged to the same effect by the Governor-General as by Lawrence, doubtfully agreed to lose no time in carrying out their policy of a march on Delhi. This is not the only instance throughout the Indian Mutiny where the hesitations and weakness of military men were happily overruled by the resolute counsels of civilians. The ordinary precautions of warfare had often to be disregarded in the struggle now at hand.

The difficulties, indeed, might well have seemed appalling. At Umballa itself, an abortive attempt at mutiny had taken place on the fatal 10th. General Anson, who, like some other Queen's officers, had hitherto been apt to despise the Sepoys, now went to the other extreme in flattering them, and let their officers hamper him by a promise that they should not be disarmed. At his back, the fashionable station of Simla was thrown into panic by a disturbance among the Goorkhas posted there. Hundreds of English people fled to the woods and mountains in terror, till it was found that the Goorkhas could easily be brought to reason. They luckily showed no fellow-feeling with the Bengal Sepoys; and soldiers from this warlike mountain race served us well throughout the Mutiny. The native princes of the neighbourhood also gave timely help of their troops and by furnishing supplies.

Within a fortnight were gathered at Umballa three English infantry regiments, the 9th Lancers, and twelve field-guns, with one regiment and one squadron of natives whom it was not safe to leave behind. Carts had been collected by the hundred, camels and elephants by the thousand, and a numerous train of camp-followers, without whom an Indian army can hardly move. Ammunition was brought up from the arsenal at Philour, one of the Punjaub strongholds, secured just in time to prevent it falling into treacherous hands. A siege-train, hastily prepared here, had to be escorted by Sepoys, who might at any moment break into revolt. The Sutlej, swollen with melting snows, threatened to break down the bridge by which communication was kept up with this important point; and, not two hours after the train had passed, the bridge in fact gave way. Then there were delays through unmanageable bullocks ploughing over heavy sands and roads deluged by rain. The first day's labour of twenty hours brought the train only seven miles on its long route.

Without waiting for it, on May 25, Anson advanced to Kurnaul, the rallying-point of the Delhi fugitives. But cholera, a feller foe than the Sepoy, had already attacked his soldiers. One of the first victims was the Commander-in-Chief, who died on the 27th, broken by ill-health and the burden of a task too heavy for him. Another kind of General, it was said by impatient critics, would have been in Delhi a week before. But this was easier to say than to do, and certainly the destruction of his small and ill-provided army, hurled forward without due precaution, might have proved the loss of India.

Anson was succeeded in command by Sir Henry Barnard, an officer of Crimean distinction, who had been only a few weeks in India. His first acts showed no want of energy. Leaving the siege-train to follow at its slow pace, he moved upon Delhi at the end of the month, his men marching eagerly under the fierce June sun, in burning desire to avenge the slaughter of their country-people. And now began those cruel reprisals by which our victory was so darkly stained. Angry suspicion was all the evidence needed to condemn the natives, guilty and innocent alike, who, after a hasty show of trial, were often mocked and tortured before execution at the hands of Christians turned into savages. The Sepoy regiment which marched with the column from Umballa had to be sent away, to protect them against the suspicious resentment of their English comrades, as much as in anticipation of the treachery which soon displayed itself among them.

A few days' march brought together the main body and Brigadier Wilson's force from Meerut, which had lain there shamefully inactive for three weeks, but now did much to retrieve its character by two encounters under such a burning sun that the exhausted soldiers could not follow up their victory. The whole army numbered little over three thousand Englishmen, with whom Barnard pushed forward to where, five miles north of Delhi, a horde of mutineers lay waiting to dispute his advance, strongly posted at Budlee-ka-Serai.

Here on June 8th was fought the first important battle of the war. Nothing could resist this handful of British soldiers, terrible in their vengeful passion. Blinded by the glare, now choked by dust, now wading knee-deep in water, through all obstacles, the infantry dashed up to the rebel guns; the Lancers, having made a stealthy circuit, charged upon the enemy's rear; the field artillery took them in the flank; and they fled in confusion, pressed hard by the eager though jaded victors. On the Ridge without the city the Sepoys made another stand, but were again swept back from this strong position. After sixteen hours' marching and fighting, under a sun whose rays were almost as fatal as bullets, the English soldiers encamped among the burned quarters of the Cantonment, and from the Ridge beheld the domes and minarets of that famous city, which already they looked upon as regained.

But not next day, as they had fondly hoped, nor next week, nor for weary months, were they to pass the high red wall and heavy bastions that defiantly confronted them. Even had those walls lain flat as Jericho's, it were madness to have thrown some couple of thousand bayonets into the narrow crooked streets of a city swarming with fanatical foemen, besides a Sepoy garrison many times the number of the assailants. Open still on all sides but one, Delhi was the rendezvous of bands of mutineers flocking into it from various quarters; from first to last it is said to have held forty thousand of them—a strange reversal of the rules of war, which require that a besieging force shall at least outnumber the besieged! Still, in the first few days, Barnard did entertain the notion of carrying the place by a *coup de main*, but allowed himself to be dissuaded, to the disgust of certain ardent and youthful spirits.

There was then nothing for it but to remain camped behind the Ridge, awaiting reinforcements and the coming up of the siege-train. In this position, the rear defended by a canal, and with a wall of rocky heights in front, our army was practically besieged rather than besieging. Their field artillery could make little impression on the walls, nearly a mile off, while the enemy's heavier guns sent shot among them night and day. So great was the want of ammunition that two annas apiece were offered for cannon balls, which natives risked their lives in picking up to be fired back into the city—balls which sometimes could hardly be handled by Europeans in the burning heat. Sunstroke struck them down as by lightning; half the officers of one regiment were thus disabled in a single day. The over-tasked force had often to fight all day and to watch all night. The enemy used his superiority of numbers by continual harassing attacks, in front, in flank, and at last in the rear. The day was a remarkable one which passed without fighting. In six weeks, twenty combats were counted. On the 23rd of June, the Centenary of Plassey, a particularly formidable assault was made, and repulsed after a long day's fighting, to the discouragement of the Sepoys, whom false prophecies had led to believe that this date was to be fatal to us. Now, as always, the skulking foe could never stand to face British bayonets in the open; but their stealthy onsets were favoured by the wilderness of tangled ravines, gardens, walls, ruins, tombs, thickets, and deserted houses, which gave them cover right up to our entrenchments.

Through the losses of these continual encounters, as well as through disease and exposure, our scanty force would soon have melted away, if reinforcements had not begun to come in towards the end of June. But now also came the rainy season, multiplying the ravages of fever and cholera. Poor General Barnard was so worn out by the strain of his almost hopeless task that he could neither eat nor sleep. Early in July he died, like his predecessor, of cholera. General Reed took up the command, but at the end of a week, finding the burden too heavy for his feeble health, gave it over to Brigadier Wilson, who at one time had almost retired in despair, and would probably have done so if not cheered and strengthened by one who, at a distance, was all along the moving spirit of this marvellous siege.

Sir John Lawrence it is, with his lieutenants, Montgomery, Herbert Edwardes, Neville Chamberlain, John Nicholson, who are on all hands hailed as foremost among the saviours of our Indian empire. The Punjaub, where Lawrence bore rule at this crisis, home of the warlike Sikhs, might have been judged our weakest point, yet he turned it into a source of strength. Our latest and hardest conquest as it was, conquerors and conquered had learned to respect one another as worthy foemen, while its manly population bore a contemptuous ill-will towards the rebel Sepoys, and, themselves divided between Sikh and Moslem, did not readily find common cause to make against the English. From this mingled population, Lawrence quickly began to enlist excellent soldiers, weeding out also the Punjaub Sepoys from the ranks of their East-country comrades, to form the nucleus of new corps. Punjaubees, Afghans, Pathans, all the most martial and restless spirits of the frontier, eagerly came forward for our service; and thus the very men from whom we had most to fear became serviceable allies in the time of need.

The old Sepoy regiments were for the most part disarmed one by one, some of them disbanded, as opportunity or suspicion counselled, yet not till more than one had made attempts at mutiny that ended ill for themselves. Lawrence, earnest in urging mercy when the time came for it, was resolute in trampling out the early sparks of disaffection. Forty mutinous Sepoys at once were blown away from the mouths of guns. The dangerous districts were scoured by a movable column under Nicholson, a man worshipped almost as a god by his Sikh followers. The Afghan frontier had also to be watched, lest old enemies there should take this chance of falling upon us from behind when our hands were so full of fighting in front. And at the same time it was necessary to keep a careful eye upon our new levies, lest they in turn should grow too formidable.

Fortunate it was that the neighbouring native princes proved friendly, lending the aid of their troops to keep the peace, or giving more substantial assistance to the representative of that power which they had learned to look upon as paramount. Lawrence, governing a population of twenty millions, cut off from communication with his superiors, was made by force of circumstances dictator of Northern India. Not for nearly three months did a message from Calcutta reach him by the circuitous way of Bombay. The generals in the field, though owing him no formal obedience, gave in to the energy of his character and the weight of his experience. The well-provided arsenals and magazines of the Punjaub, saved from the hands of the mutineers by his vigorous action, became now the base of supplies against Delhi. Thither he kept forwarding a continual stream of stores, transport, men and money, which he had to raise by somewhat forced loans among the rich natives. Thus, in spite of a painful ailment, in spite of his longing for home and rest, he throughout masterfully maintained the British prestige within his own boundaries, while ever pressing on the capture of Delhi, as the blow which would paralyze rebellion all over India. When the great enterprise seemed on the point of failure, as a last resource he sent Nicholson's column to the front, leaving himself with only four thousand European soldiers scattered among the millions of the Punjaub, for whom that one man's strong hand was equal to a host of fighters.

Still the siege of Delhi dragged on its costly length. We must leave it for the meanwhile to see what thrilling and momentous scenes were being enacted in other parts of India, and to follow the preparations made for attacking the mutiny from the further side.

Calcutta was in a state of bewildered dismay, not to be calmed by official hopes for a speedy end to the insurrection, and soon increasing daily with worse and worse news from up-country. From Allighur, from Muttra, from Bareilly, from Moradabad, from Jhansi, from other points, one after another, came sickening tales of revolt and massacre, which would not lose in the telling. The only news of other places was an ominous silence. The great stations of Agra, Cawnpore, and Lucknow were presently cut off by a raging sea of rebellion. Rohilcund, old nursery of warriors, was overflowed, and the Doab, that fertile region between the Jumna and the Ganges, down whose thickly peopled valleys poured the irresistible flood of disorder. The tide rose to the sacred cities of Allahabad and Benares. Beyond, there were risings in Rajpootana. At Gwalior, the Maharajah's Sepoy contingent, after a time, broke away to play a considerable part in coming battles. Everywhere regiments, believed faithful, were going off like the guns of a burning ship.

The leaven of agitation naturally spread into the two other Presidencies, where the English officials could have no quiet rest till the danger in Bengal should be over. But the organization of the Madras and Bombay armies was not so dangerous for their rulers. Here men of various creeds and castes were more thoroughly mixed together in the ranks, which in Bengal had been allowed to consist too much of fellow-believers, and of cliques of the same family, caste or locality, turning every company into a clan animated by a common feeling apart from that of soldierly duty; nor, outside of Bengal, were the regiments permitted to be accompanied by squalid fakirs, to keep alive their superstitious zeal.

When Patna and Dinapore gave signs of commotion, not four hundred miles from Calcutta, the people of the capital might well look to see peril at their doors. They loudly accused Lord Canning as wanting to the exigency. He certainly seemed to go too far in trying to allay alarm by putting a calm face upon his inward anxiety. He forbore, as long as possible, to show distrust of the Sepoys in Eastern Bengal; he hesitated about accepting a contingent of Goorkhas offered him from Nepaul; he delayed in letting the inhabitants arm for their own defence. Not for a month did he allow them to form volunteer corps, and at the same time was forced to disarm the Sepoys at the neighbouring stations of Dum-Dum and Barrackpore. But rumours of what the Sepoys there had intended were already at work, producing a panic through Calcutta, where one Sunday in the middle of June a great part of the Europeans and Eurasians hastened to barricade themselves in their houses, or fled to the fort and the shipping for refuge from an imaginary foe, while the poor natives lay hid, trembling on their own account, expecting quite as groundlessly to be massacred by the white soldiers. The ludicrous terror of this "Panic Sunday" will long be remembered as a joke against the Calcutta people, who only towards evening began to see they had nothing to fear. Next day their restored confidence was strengthened by the arrest of the King of Oudh, who held a quasi-state in his palace near the city, and whose retainers were believed to have been plotting, with the now harmless Sepoys at the neighbouring stations, for a great Christian massacre.

A day or two later, Sir Patrick Grant, Commander of the Madras army, arrived to assume command in Bengal. He did not feel himself equal to taking the field in person, but made the fortunate choice of Brigadier-General Havelock to advance against the rebels, as soon as there should be an army ready to lead. The officer, who during the last months of his life was to burst forth as a popular hero, had passed obscurely a long life of eastern military service. In India, indeed, he was well known for the earnest piety which had leavened the ranks of his comrades. "Havelock's Saints," a name given in mockery, became a title of honour, when it was found that the little band among whom he preached and prayed so zealously were the best and most trustworthy soldiers of the regiment. By his superiors he had been recognized as a brave and intelligent officer; and he had served creditably in Burma, in Afghanistan, in the Punjaub, and in Persia, without attracting much public notice or rising to high command. Now, at length, this saintly veteran, all his life a careful student of the art of war, had the chance to show what he was as a general; but not till June 25 could he leave Calcutta, picking up as he went the scattered fragments of his force, which had been pushed on to meet immediate needs of succour.

A month earlier, Neill with the 1st Madras Fusiliers had gone on as forerunner of the help that would by and by be pouring in to the rescue of our imperilled countrymen. As far as Allahabad he could travel by railway, yet he did not arrive there for nearly three weeks, delayed through turning aside to repress mutiny at Benares, and by making grim examples to teach the cowering natives that the British *raj* was still to be feared. At Allahabad he found his presence sorely needed by a handful of Europeans shut up in the fort along with a band of hardly controllable Sikhs. The mutiny here had been marked by painful as well as curious features. The Sepoys at first showed themselves enthusiastically loyal, giving every sign of affection to their officers, then rose against them in a sudden fit of cruel fury, immediately after volunteering, with apparent heartiness, to march against their comrades at Delhi. Seven or eight boy-ensigns were murdered by the regiment they had just joined. The rebels bombarded the locomotives on the new railway, which they took for mysterious engines of warfare. There were the usual sickening massacres of women and children. A general destruction had reigned without check, in which helpless Hindoo pilgrims came off almost as ill as the Christians at the hands of a Mohamedan mob. This short triumph of disorder was with terrible and too little discriminating justice chastised by Neill, stern Scotchman that he was. What between the mutineers and the British soldiery, the inhabitants of the district had cause to rue these troubles; and again our civilization was disgraced by a blind fury of vengeance. Neill was more successful in restoring order among the populace than in restraining his own soldiers, who gave way to excesses of drink that fatally nursed the seeds of cholera, when not a man could be spared from the trying task before them.[2]

By the end of June, Havelock reached Allahabad, to take the head of an army that hardly numbered two thousand fighters. Nineteen officers and men made all his cavalry. But such news here met him, he could not lose a day in flinging this small force among myriads of bitter foes, at whose mercy lay the lives of many

[2] One of the severest punishments inflicted on mutineers was forcing them under the lash, before being hanged, to sweep up the blood of their supposed victims, so as, in their ideas, to pollute them to all eternity. A generation later, this General Neill's son was murdered, it is said, by the vengeful son of a native officer thus punished.

Christian women and children. Yet it was no horde of undisciplined savages from whom he must wrest those hapless captives. Throughout the war, our troops had to face, at enormous odds of number, ranks trained and armed by ourselves, supplied from our own captured stores, and in a large degree led by the establishment of native officers whom we had taught how battles should be won. Never perhaps has it been so well proved, as by the result of this apparently unequal conflict, what advantage lies in pride and strength of race!

# CHAPTER V

## THE CITIES OF REFUGE

Minor disturbances on the outskirts left out of sight, the stress of the storm may now be considered as confined to the region between Delhi and Allahabad, where in Agra, Cawnpore, and Lucknow were still havens of refuge, that, it was to be feared, could not long hold out against the turbulent elements surging around and against them.

At Agra, one of the most magnificent cities in India, and the seat of the Government of the North-Western Provinces, there reigned the liveliest alarm among the large Christian community, though Lieutenant-Governor Colvin at first tried to make too light of the danger. When the neighbouring stations burst into mutiny, a panic set in, the Sepoys were disarmed, and by the end of June the Europeans took refuge within the high red walls of the fort, some mile and a half in circuit, that enclose a strangely-mingled maze of buildings, galleries, pavilions, domes, towers, vaults, offices, barracks, arcades, gardens and lordly halls recalling the Arabian Nights, among them such architectural wonders as the glittering palace of Akbar and the exquisite Pearl Mosque, now turned into a hospital for the nonce. In sight of these monuments of Mogul grandeur, a mile or so up the Jumna, rise the snowy splendours of the Taj, that Sultana's tomb praised by some as the most beautiful work of human hands; and on this side, without the city, were the English homes that must be deserted as insecure. The citadel of Agra now gave quarters to several thousand persons, the number increasing as destitute fugitives came slinking in from the wrecked stations around. There was an English regiment here, and a small force of volunteers, who, in July, sallied out to meet a Sepoy army, but had to retire with some loss; then the unfortunate refugees found themselves forced helplessly to look on at the burning of their houses without the walls, while thousands of prisoners, released from the jail, spread over the country in their clanking chains, and for a few days the *budmashes* and the rabble had their way in the city. No vigorous attempt, however, was made to besiege the Fort, and its inmates got off with the half-serious, half-ludicrous hardships of an anxious summer spent in marble halls and crowded palace-chambers, where decorations of mosaic, enamel and coloured glass ill made up for the lack of substantial comfort.

Poor Colvin, broken down, like so many another leader of that time, by the burden of a charge too heavy for him, and pained by the quarrels and murmurs of the pent-up multitude under his too feeble authority, died in September, yet not till he had seen the motley garrison venturing forth again, and beginning to restore order in the districts about. On the whole, the story of Agra was rather a happily prosaic one for a scene of such picturesque historic grandeur.

**Taj of Agra, from the Fountain.**

At Meerut also, where the Mutiny first broke out, our people got through its further alarms by standing on anxious guard behind their entrenchments, while Dunlop the magistrate, at the news of trouble hurrying back from his holiday in the Himalayas, raised a force of volunteers that by their bold sallies kept the disaffected in awe for some way round.

Very different was the case of Lucknow, capital of Oudh, a vast expanse of hovels and palaces, situated on the banks of the Goomtee, amid a rich country famed as the garden of India. With its straggling suburbs, it covered a space six miles long and about half as broad, including groups of stately temples, palaces and pleasure-gardens. The central part of the city was densely populated, and the chief streets offered a lively scene, thronged as they were with natives in the picturesque costumes of all parts of India, with rich palanquins, with stately elephants, and camels in gay caparisons, with gorgeously-attired cavaliers and their swaggering attendants. Every man in those days went armed, frays and outrages being too common under the weak tyranny of the lately deposed sovereign; even beggars demanded charity almost at the point of the sword, and it was a point of prudence as well as of honour for every dignitary to surround himself with a retinue of formidable warriors.

Over this swarm of dangerous elements Sir Henry Lawrence now held rule, worthy brother of the Punjaub administrator. There were four Lawrence brothers, who all manfully played parts in the Mutiny. Among them Henry seems to have been the most lovable, distinguished as a philanthropist not less than as a statesman and a soldier. The institutions which he founded for the education of soldiers' children in India still attest his benevolence towards his own people. He had singular sympathy with and knowledge of the natives, yet there was no sentimentalism in his earnest desire for their welfare, and when the time came for stern repression he would not shrink from the uncongenial task. On the earliest disturbances, he telegraphed to Calcutta asking to be invested with full powers to deal with them; then, prematurely aged as he was by hard work and sickness, strained every nerve to meet the emergency, which seems to have taken him not so much by surprise as in the case of other high officers.

Discontent was strong in the newly-annexed kingdom of Oudh; and already had Lawrence had to quell an attempt at mutiny caused by the greased cartridges, before the native troops raised the standard of rebellion at Delhi. Foreboding the worst from the news of what had happened on the Jumna, he exerted himself to calm and conciliate the Sepoys at Lucknow, and for a time succeeded in preserving an appearance of order, under which, however, the signs of mischief brewing did not escape his watchful eye. The Residency, his palatial quarters, with the public offices and houses about it, stood upon a slight rising ground near the river, overlooking the greater part of the city. From the first, Lawrence began to turn this position into a fort of refuge, storing here guns, ammunition, and supplies, as also in the Muchee Bhawun, an imposing native fortress not far off. For garrison, part of the 32nd Regiment, the only English troops he had, were moved in from their Cantonments outside, and the Christian population soon abandoned their homes for the asylum of the Residency. Yet at this time it was in no state for serious defence; even weeks later, few foresaw the hot siege it would undergo. Before long there appeared cause for actively pushing on the work. Early in May there was a mutinous demonstration that luckily could be appeased without bloodshed, but it too plainly showed the temper of the Sepoys.

By the end of the month, the women and children were all ordered in from the Cantonments. Business was now at a standstill, and English people venturing into the streets met everywhere with scared as well as scowling faces, many of the better class fearing to lose the safety of our Government, while the turbulent elements of the population eagerly awaited the signal for general lawlessness.

Sir Henry Lawrence has been blamed because, like other leaders on whom rested the same responsibility, he delayed to disarm the Sepoy regiments at Lucknow, fearing chiefly to bring about the mutiny of others who, at various points in Oudh, still openly obeyed their officers. Holding to his policy of pretended confidence, on May 30th he was warned that a general mutiny would break out at evening gun-fire. He went to dine in the Cantonments, as if no danger were to be feared; and at the report of the nine o'clock gun, he remarked with a smile to his informant, "Your friends are not punctual." But scarcely were the words out of his mouth than a crackle of musketry came from the lines. Calmly ordering his native guard to load, though for all he knew it might be to shoot him on the spot, Lawrence hastened to overawe their mutinous comrades. Only one whole regiment had broken out, most of whose officers had time to escape with their lives. The Sepoys, however, shot their brigadier as he tried to recall them to obedience, and two other Englishmen were murdered, one a young cornet of seventeen lying sick in his bungalow. For this small bloodshed the mutineers consoled themselves by burning and plundering the abandoned bungalows, till Lawrence came upon them at the head of an English detachment, before whom they soon took to flight, yet not till the firing and glare had spread wide alarm among the Europeans.

Of the two other Sepoy regiments, some five or six hundred men fell in under their officers' orders; the rest kept out of the way, or went off to the mutineers. Next morning, Lawrence followed them on to the race-course, where they had retreated, and they fled afresh from the English artillery, though not till the fugitive Sepoys had been joined by the greater part of a cavalry regiment, for want of whom effectual pursuit could not be made. In the course of the day there was an abortive mob-rising within the city, easily put down by the native police, a number of insurgents being captured and executed.

The English leaders tried to encourage themselves by the thought that this long-dreaded mine had gone off with so little mischief, and that now, at least, they knew their friends from their enemies. But they did not foresee how fast would spread the madness which in so many cases suddenly affected bodies hitherto faithful even against their own comrades. A few days later, the police also mutinied and made off, pursued by artillery, and a force of volunteer cavalry hastily raised among the Europeans. Still a few hundred Sepoys, who had stuck to their colours, were stationed beside English soldiers at the Residency and the Muchee Bhawun; and, on an appeal to their loyalty, a considerable number of old native pensioners, some of them blind and crippled, presented themselves to stand by the Government whose salt they had eaten so long.

Among the reminiscences of that trying time, young readers will be especially interested in those of Mr. E.H. Hilton, an Eurasian gentleman still living in Lucknow, to show with pride the carbine he bore as a school-boy through the siege, and to say *quaeque ipse miserrima vidi,* if he remember as much from school-books, which may well have been driven out of his head by the experiences of his last days at school.

Mr. Hilton, then well on in his teens, was in 1857 one of the senior boys of the Martinière College, at which his parents held the posts of Sergeant-Superintendent and Matron. This institution, also known as Constantia House, from the motto *Labore et Constantia* inscribed on its front, is one of the lions of Lucknow. Founded at the beginning of our century by General Claude Martin, a French soldier of fortune, it has given a good education to thousands of European and half-caste boys; nor is this the only educational endowment due to his munificence. The Martinière, as it is commonly called, a huge, fantastic, straggling mansion in a pleasant park some mile or two out of the city, was the founder's residence during his lifetime, and afterwards his monument and tomb, for he had himself buried in a vault below the spacious halls and dormitories, now alive with the lads whom that singular Frenchman had at heart to educate in the English language and religion. At the time of the Mutiny, there were sixty-five resident pupils, who had naturally to share the forebodings and alarms of that terrible spring.

When all the other Christians stood on their guard, Mr. Schilling, Principal of the Martinière, prepared to defend his charge against any sudden attack. A small party, first of Sepoys, and when they could no longer be trusted, of English soldiers, was stationed at the College. The elder boys were armed with muskets or carbines. Stores of food and water were collected; and Mr. Hilton tells us how the first taste his school-fellows had of the trials of the Mutiny was the frequent bursting of earthen water-jars, which drenched the boys in the dormitory below. The centre of the building was barricaded with bricks, sand-bags, boxes of old books and crockery, anything that could be turned to account. The boys still did their school-work in the long open wings, but with orders to make for the centre, thus turned into a citadel, as soon as the alarm-bell rang. One boy always stood on the look-out; and, as may be supposed, there were several false alarms, when a troop of grass-cutters' ponies, or the dark edge of a dust-storm was taken by the nervous young sentinels for an advancing army.

These lads were, indeed, in an exposed position, where they could not long hope to hold out against soldiers, but might have beaten off a sudden attack from the rabble of Lucknow. When the bungalows were burned, young Hilton had nearly seen too much of that night's work. He had gone, as usual, in charge of a party of his school-fellows, who acted as choir-boys of the English Church, riding to and fro, it seems, upon nothing less than elephants!

"We were in the midst of chanting the *Magnificat,* when suddenly the bugles sounded the alarm. All the officers present quietly rose up and marched out, and, after finishing the *Magnificat,* the service was then suddenly brought to a close. The

Rev. Mr. Polehampton took the choir-boys to his house, and gave us the choice of remaining there or proceeding to the Martinière at once. As our elephants were waiting ready, I preferred to take the boys home, and we twelve set off on our moonlight journey of about six miles. Near the Iron Bridge, we passed a regiment of Sepoys marching with fixed bayonets, but, to our great relief, they took no notice of us whatever. At the Huzrutgunge Gate, opposite what is now Eduljee's shop, a sowar, with his sword drawn, rode up and ordered our *mahout* to stop. Seeing, however, that his horse would not come near our elephant, I told the *mahout* to go on. After a little colloquial abuse between the two, the *mahout* went on; the obstructive sowar took his departure with a few farewell flourishes of his naked sword, and we arrived at the Martinière without further molestation. There we found every one on the top of the building looking at the far-off flames of the burning bungalows in the Cantonments, and we received the hearty congratulations of all on what they considered our providential escape."

After the mutiny of the police, a flying skirmish took place in view of the Martinière, eagerly watched by the pupils, who were eager to join in the fray, but had to remain on guard over their buildings. Their Principal made a narrow escape, meeting the rebels as he drove through the College-park, and getting away from them by the speed of his horse. There is another story, perhaps a distorted version of the same, that one of the teachers did fall into the hands of some stragglers, who seemed inclined to shoot him, but contemptuously let him go as "only a school-master!" These school-masters, and some of the school-boys too, were to play the warrior before long.

Next morning, Mr. Schilling was ordered to abandon the College, and move his boys into the Residency. A party of the 32nd leading the way, and the elder lads with their muskets bringing up the rear, they marched through the streets lined with sullen faces, where several natives were seen going armed, but no one offered them any opposition. At the Residency they were quartered uncomfortably enough in the house of a native banker within the lines, and there went on with their lessons as best they could for two or three weeks longer.

All our people had now to take shelter behind the still imperfect defences. Large stores of food, fodder, and fire had been laid in. Fortunately there were wells of good water within the Residency entrenchment. Gunpowder and treasure were buried underground for safety. Much against his will, Lawrence gave orders for demolishing the houses around that might afford cover to assailants, but, ever anxious to spare the feelings of the natives, he desired that their holy places should be left untouched, so that the adjacent mosques remained to be used as works for the besiegers. The preparations, within and without, of the garrison were far from complete by the end of June, when cholera and small-pox appeared among them, to add to the gloom of their prospects. The buildings about the Residency were now crowded with people, not only the whole English population of Lucknow, but refugees from out-stations, who kept coming in for their lives. The worst tidings reached them from all hands. No sign of help cleared the threatening horizon. It was still open to Lawrence to abandon the city, retreating under protection of his one European regiment and his guns. But he took the boldest for the best policy, and kept the British flag floating over its capital when all the rest of Oudh was in unrestrained rebellion.

He even judged himself strong enough, or was unluckily persuaded, to strike a blow outside his defences. Hearing that the vanguard of a Sepoy army had reached Chinhut, a few miles from Lucknow, on the last day of June, he marched out against them with some seven hundred men, hoping to scatter the mutineers before they could enter the city. But, unexpectedly, he found himself assailed by overwhelming numbers, for he had been deceived through false information, and it was a whole army, not their mere advance guard, with which he had to do. The European soldiers could not long hold out under a burning sun, when the native cavalry and gunners either fled or went over to the enemy. The retreat became a shameful rout. The broken band was almost surrounded, and owed its escape to the gallant charge made by a handful of mounted volunteers, most of whom here saw their first battle. The water-carriers, such indispensable attendants in this climate, having deserted, our men suffered agonies from thirst, and many more might have perished if the inhabitants had not come out to offer them water, showing that we had still some friends left. But as Lawrence galloped on, heavy-hearted, to break the bad news to those left behind in the Residency, already he found the native population in hasty flight; and soon an ominous silence made the streets outside our entrenchments like a city of the dead. It grew lively enough later in the day, when the victorious Sepoys came pouring in, and then began the long misery of the defence of Lucknow.

But that renowned episode shall be treated of in a chapter apart. For the present we pass on to Cawnpore, where another wretched crowd were already undergoing the horrors of a siege, and had earnestly begged from Lucknow the help it could not spare. Their sufferings and fate should be fully told, as an epitome of the Mutiny's most painful features.

Cawnpore, though no such splendid historic city as Delhi or Lucknow, was an important military station, with a force of some three hundred English soldiers, counting officers and invalids, to ten times as many Sepoys. At Bithoor, about twelve miles up the Ganges, was the palace of that wily and cruel Hindoo who, under the title of Nana Sahib, became so widely known as the villain of a great tragedy. Adopted son of the dethroned Mahratta potentate entitled the Peshwa, and left a rich man by inheriting his wealth, he had a grievance against our Government in its refusal to continue to him the ample pension paid to the late Peshwa, whose heir by adoption, by foul play if all stories are true, was, however, recognized as Maharajah of Bithoor, and allowed to keep up a sumptuous court among some hundreds of idle and insolent retainers. To ventilate his wrongs, Nana Sahib sent to England a confidential agent named Azimoolah, a low-born adventurer like himself, who by dint of shrewdness and impudence made an extraordinary impression on London society. This part of his career reads like a comic romance, and seems indeed to have suggested to Thackeray the Rummun Loll of *The Newcomes*. But, though petted and flattered by English fine ladies, Azimoolah could get no satisfaction from men in office; then returned to his employer, during the Crimean War, with a report that England was likely to be humbled by Russia.

The Nana dissembled his resentment, and appeared to have given himself up to a life of pleasure, in which degrading Oriental sensualities were strangely mixed with an affectation of European tastes. Yet, while pretending friendship with the English, and leading them to think him a good-natured, jovial fellow, whose main ambition was to cultivate their society, this dissembler, it seems, secretly nursed the blackest hatred against his neighbours and frequent guests, biding a time when he might satisfy the grudge he bore against their race.

That startling news from Meerut had found our people at Cawnpore engaged in the tedious round of duty, and the languid efforts to kill time, which make the life of Anglo-Indians not lucky enough to get away for the hot weather to bracing hill-stations. Henceforth, they could not complain of any want of excitement. They had plenty of time for preparation to meet the danger, for three weeks passed before it was upon them.

The General in command here, Sir Hugh Wheeler, was an Indian veteran of the older school, who could speak to the Sepoys in their own language, and, like some other officers of his generation, had become so much one of themselves as to marry a native woman. Such a man would naturally be slow to believe his "children"—*babalogue* the affectionate word was, that came now to be used rather in scornful irony—capable of being untrue to their salt. Yet when the demeanour of the Sepoys, agitated as much by fear and unreasoning excitement, perhaps, as by deliberate intention to revolt, became too plainly threatening, while still expressing confidence, Wheeler ordered an entrenchment to be thrown up and provided with stores, as a refuge for the Europeans in case of need. So great was his trust in the Maharajah of Bithoor, that he did not doubt to accept the Nana's assistance. A detachment of his ragamuffin troops was actually put in charge of the treasury; and there was some talk of the ladies and children being placed for safety in the palace of this traitor, already plotting their ruin. Every night now they slept within the entrenchment; but the officers of Sepoy regiments had to show true courage by staying among their men, who were not so much impressed by this forced show of confidence as by the distrust of them evident in the preparations for defence.

At length even Sir Hugh began to take a gloomy view of the situation. Many of those under him had done so from the first; and most pathetic it is to read the letters written by some English people to their friends at home by the last mail that got down to Calcutta—farewell messages of men and women who felt how any hour now they might be called on to face death. Before long the roads were all stopped, the telegraph wires were cut, and almost the only news that reached this blockaded garrison of what went on around them, was the grim hint conveyed by white corpses floating down the sacred river, like an offering to cruel Hindoo gods.

On the night of June 4 came the long-expected outbreak. Part of the Sepoys gave themselves up to the usual outrages, breaking open the jail, plundering the treasury and the magazine. The rest remained quiet for a time, and one regiment was even falling in upon the *maidan* to obey its officers, when, with ill-starred haste, Sir Hugh Wheeler had them fired on from the entrenchment, at which they ran away to join the mutineers. About eighty, however, were found obstinately faithful. More than one of the native officers also risked his life in trying to restrain his men; but others sided with the revolt, among them a Soubahdar named Teeka Singh, who became its general, the Nana Sahib being adopted as a figure-head. He at once consented to lead them to Delhi, and the whole disorderly crew had marched off on the road, when his crafty counsellor, Azimoolah, is understood to have persuaded him that instead of going to swell the triumph of a Moslem king, it would be more to his glory and profit to exterminate the English at Cawnpore, and set up a Brahmin power of his own. The Nana, in turn, won over the Sepoys to this view, and next morning they marched back upon the entrenchment at Cawnpore.

The English here had been fondly hoping the danger past with the running away of their Sepoys, and congratulated themselves that, no longer tied by duty, they would now be able to make their escape down the river. What was their consternation when that trusted friend of theirs unmasked himself by sending in to General Wheeler a note, bidding him to expect an immediate attack! At hasty notice, they fled within the entrenchment, some just in time; others, lingering or trusting to concealment, were butchered by the desperadoes, who soon filled the streets to make themselves a terror to respectable natives as well as to Europeans. The strength of the disorder here was among the Hindoos, at whose hands the Mohamedans were like to come ill-off; and if they had not been united by a common hatred, they would probably before long have taken to cutting one another's throats.

After spending the forenoon in pillage, murder, and arson, the rebel army came forward to the bombardment of that weak entrenchment, which was to endure a siege seldom surpassed for misery and disaster. Sir Hugh Wheeler is judged to have made a fatal mistake in not possessing himself of the magazine, a strong position, which, with all its contents, he abandoned, rather than irritate the Sepoys by taking it out of their hands, and thus, perhaps, drive them into revolt. He seems not to have reckoned on any serious attack. The fortress he had provided was the buildings of a hospital and some unfinished barracks, surrounded by a low mud wall, standing out in the open plain, and commanded on all sides by substantial edifices, at a few hundred yards' distance, to give cover for the besiegers, who soon surrounded it with batteries of our own heavy guns, while the defenders had mounted only a few nine-pounders. Within such slight defences were huddled some thousand Christian souls, four hundred of them fighting men. They had plenty of muskets and rifles, but sorely needed every other means of defence.

For now broke over these poor people a storm of cannon-balls and bullets, pouring upon them all day like the slaughtering rays of the sun overhead, and hardly ceasing by night, when they must steal forth in wary silence to hide away their dead. At first every crashing shot called forth shrieks of alarm from the women and children; but soon they grew too well accustomed to the deadly din. In two or three days all the buildings which gave them shelter were riddled through and through. There was no part of the enclosure where flying missiles and falling brickwork did not work havoc, as well as upon the thin circle of defenders exposing themselves behind the wretched walls. By the end of a week all the artillerymen had been killed or wounded beside their ill-protected guns. But the sick, too, were put out of pain, in whatever corners they might be laid. Children fell dead at play, their mothers in nursing them. One shot struck down husband, wife and child at once. Another carried off the head of General Wheeler's sick son, before the eyes of his horrified family. Two men and seven women were the victims of a single shell. An important out-work was the unfinished barrack, garrisoned by less than a score of men, few of whom ever left that post unhurt. Yet all did their duty as manfully as if not robbed by continual alarms of their nightly rest, with brave hearts tormented night and day by fear for their patient dear ones.

Foremost among so many heroes was Captain Moore of the 32nd, who seems to have been looked on as the soul of the defence, ever present at the sorest need, and never seen but to leave "men something more courageous, and women something less unhappy." We recognize another Greatheart of a different order in Mr. Moncrieff, the chaplain, unsparing of himself to cheer the living and soothe the dying with words to which none now could listen in careless ease. Few and short, indeed, were the prayers which that Christian flock could make over their dead, stealthily buried by night in an empty well without the rampart. Another well within proved more perilous than that of Bethlehem, from which David longed to drink. This was the garrison's one supply of water, and the ruthless enemy trained guns upon it, firing even by night as soon as they heard the creaking of the tackle. When the Hindoo water-carriers had all been killed, or scared away, soldiers were paid several rupees for every pail they drew at the risk of their lives. A brave civilian named Mackillop, declaring himself no fighting man, undertook this post of honour, held only for a few days. In the heat of June, on that dusty plain, no fainting woman or crying child could have a drink of water, but at the price of blood. Washing was out of the question—a severe hardship in such a climate.

Water was not the sole want of our country-people, to many of whom the Indian summer had hitherto seemed scarcely endurable through the help of ice, effervescing beverages, apartments darkened and artificially cooled. After a week, the thatched roof of their largest building was set on fire by night, its helpless inmates hardly saved amid a shower of bullets poured on the space lit up by the flames. With this was destroyed the store of drugs and surgical instruments, so that little henceforth could be done for the sick and wounded. Another time the wood-work of a gun kindled close to the store of ammunition; then young Lieutenant Delafosse, exposing himself to the cannon turned upon this perilous spot, lay down beneath the blazing carriage, tore out the fire, and stifled it with earth before it could spread.

Many of that crowd had now to lie in the open air, or in what holes and corners they could find for shade, exposed to the sun, and threatened by the approach of the rainy season. A plague of flies made not the least of the sufferings by which some were driven mad. They found the stench of dead animals almost intolerable. Their provisions soon began to run short; they were put on scanty rations of bad flour and split-peas. Now and then, sympathizing or calculating townsfolk managed to smuggle to them by night a basket of bread or some bottles of milk, but such god-sends would not go far among so many. A mongrel dog, a stray horse, a vagrant sacred bull, venturing near the entrenchment, was sure to fall a welcome prey. But no expedient could do more than stave off the starvation close at hand for them. Worst of all, the ammunition was not inexhaustible. Such balls as they had would no longer fit the worn-out guns. Then the ladies offered their stockings to be filled with shot. But guns failed before cartridges. At length there were only two left serviceable, when a quarter of the defenders had perished, and still the foe rained death all around the frail refuge, of which one who saw it a few weeks later says: "I could not have believed that any human beings could have stood out for one day in such a place. The walls, inside and out, were riddled with shot; you could hardly put your hand on a clear spot. The ditch and wall—it is absurd to call it a fortification—any child could have jumped over; and yet behind these for three weeks the little force held their own." This is the report of Lady Inglis, herself fresh from the perils of Lucknow, which she judged slight in proportion.

Several times dashing sorties were made to silence the most troublesome batteries, or drive away the marksmen who swarmed like rats in adjacent buildings. Thrice the enemy emboldened themselves to an assault, which was easily repulsed, though under the shelter of cotton-bales, pushed before them, a number of Sepoys contrived to advance close up to the entrenchment. They were better served by their spies, who let them know how losses and starvation must soon give the garrison into their hands without any cost of onslaught. One after another of our men stole out in disguise, vainly commissioned to seek help from Allahabad. Most of these emissaries were caught and ill-treated. More than one native messenger did get through to Lucknow; but with a sore heart Sir Henry Lawrence had to deny the appeal of his beleaguered countrymen, knowing by this time that it was all he could do to hold his own. The only reinforcement that reached Cawnpore was one young officer, who came galloping through the fire of the enemy, and leaped the wall to bring the news how his comrades had failed to make the same lucky escape. Other fugitives, seeking this poor place of refuge, were murdered on the way. Meanwhile, the ranks of the besiegers were daily swollen by all the scoundrelism of the district and by the followers of rebellious chiefs, eager to avenge the wrongs of their subjection to British rule.

Yet with them also things went not so smoothly as at first. The booty, over which they were apt to quarrel, began to be exhausted. The Sepoys could hardly be brought to face the wall of fire that ever girdled their desperate victims. The dissensions among rival believers grew strong. Their leader, jealous and suspicious of the increasing power of the Moslem party, was impatient to seal his authority in the blood of those stubborn Christians. Force failing so long, he fell back on treachery. When the siege had lasted three weeks, the garrison received a grandiloquent summons from Nana Sahib, proposing surrender on condition of receiving a safe passage to Allahabad.

General Wheeler was inclined to scorn this offer; but Moore and others, who had well earned the right to advise prudence, urged that no chivalrous pride should prevent them considering the inevitable fate of so many non-combatants. Their provisions were almost at an end. Trust in such an enemy might be doubtful, but it was the one hope of life for the women and children, if no relief came, and whence could it come? Had they only themselves to care for, these officers might have cut a way through their mutinous Sepoys. As it was, they stooped to negotiate, and on June 26th agreed to deliver up their battered works and guns, the Nana consenting that they should march out under arms, and promising means of conveyance and victuals to carry them down the river. The only difficulty was a demand on his part to take possession the same night; but when the English plenipotentiaries threatened to blow up their magazine rather, he gave in to let them wait till next morning. Through the night he was busy with his cruel counsellors, and to one named Tantia Topee, afterwards better known as a rebel general, he committed the execution of the blackest plot in this dark history.

That night our country-people slept their first quiet sleep for long, which to most of them was to be their last on earth. To some this strange stillness seemed disquieting after the din of three dreadful weeks. Early in the morning, gathering up what valuables and relics of the terrible sojourn could be borne away, they left their ruined abode with mingled emotions, on litters, carriages, and elephants, or marching warily in front and rear of the long train, were escorted down to the river by soldiers, now the Nana's, lately their own, amid a vast crowd of half-scowling, half-wondering natives. The Ghaut, or landing-steps, lay nearly a mile off, approached through the dry bed of a torrent lined at its mouth with houses and timber. About this hollow way Tantia Topee had concealed hundreds of men and several guns. As soon as the head of that slow procession reached the river-side, a bugle sounded, a line of Sepoys closed the head of the ravine to cut off retreat, and from every point of cover there broke forth a murderous roar as thousands of balls and bullets were hailed upon the entrapped crowd below.

The embarkation had already begun; the foremost of the English had laid their arms in the boats, and taken off their coats to the work; the wounded and children were being lifted on board and placed under the thatched roofs of these clumsy vessels. But at that signal the boatmen had all deserted, after setting the thatch on fire, and some unhappy creatures were burned to death, while others plunged into the water, vainly seeking escape from the balls splashing around them. On land also a fearful slaughter was going on. Some of the Englishmen tried to return the fire; some laboured to push off the boats, which had purposely been stuck fast in the sand. Only three were launched, one of which drifted across to the opposite bank, and there fell into the hands of another band of slaughterers. The second appears to have made a little way down the river before being disabled by a round shot. The third got off clear, floating along the sluggish current, a target for ambushed cannon and musketry, through which swam several brave men, some to sink beneath the reddened stream, some to reach that sole ark of deliverance. The rest remained at the traitor's mercy. After most of them had been shot down, their false escort of troopers dashed into the water to finish the bloody work, stabbing women and tearing children in pieces. The General was butchered here, with his young daughter, unless, as would appear from some accounts, Sir Hugh survived in a dying state on board the escaped boat. Here died the chaplain, beginning a prayer. A whole girls' school and their mistress perished wretchedly. Nearly five hundred in all must have fallen on the banks or in that fatal ravine, when a messenger arrived from the Nana, ordering to kill the men, but to spare such women and children as still survived. A hundred and twenty-five, half dead with terror, drenched with mud and blood, were collected from the carnage and brought to Cawnpore.

The one boat which had escaped was crowded with about a hundred persons, dead and living, including some of the chief heroes of the defence. There is no more thrilling tale in fiction than the adventures of that hopeless crew. They had no oars; their rudder was soon broken by a shot. Paddling with bits of plank, they slowly drifted down the Ganges, fired at from either bank. More than once they stuck fast in the sand, and at night the women had to be disembarked before the cumbrous craft could be got off. By daylight they had come only a few miles from Cawnpore. Again were they attacked from the bank, and found themselves pursued by a boat filled with armed men. The torrential rains of an Indian summer burst upon them. They were obliged to tear off the thatched roof of the boat, as the enemy had tried to set it on fire. The second night found them helplessly aground; but a hurricane came to their aid, and the boat floated off before morning, only to drift into a backwater. There they grounded once more, and the enemy soon gathered about them in overpowering numbers.

Some dozen men, under Lieutenant Mowbray Thomson, waded on shore to beat back the assailants, while the rest made an effort to shove off the boat. This little party, sent out on what seemed a forlorn hope, in the end furnished the only survivors; their leader was one of four who lived to tell the tale. Desperately charging the mob of Sepoys and peasants on the bank, they drove them back for some distance, but soon found themselves surrounded by overwhelming numbers. Without the loss of a man, however, though not without wounds, they cut their way back to the shore, to find the boat gone. Expecting to catch it up, they pushed on down the stream, but could see nothing of it, and had to shift for themselves as best they could. Spread out in open order to give less mark for bullets, they held together, loading and firing upon the rabble that pressed at their heels, yet not too near, like a cowardly pack of wolves. When the hunted Englishmen had toiled some two or three miles barefoot over rough ground, a temple appeared in the distance, for which the officer shaped his course. Mowbray Thomson himself, in his *Story of Cawnpore*, describes the last stand made here by this remnant of its garrison.

"I instantly set four of the men crouching in the doorway with bayonets fixed, and their muskets so placed as to form a *cheval-de-frise* in the narrow entrance. The mob came on helter-skelter, in such maddening haste that some of them fell or were pushed on to the bayonets, and their transfixed bodies made the barrier impassable to the rest, upon whom we, from behind our novel defence, poured shot upon shot into the crowd. The situation was the more favourable to us, in consequence of the temple having been built upon a base of brickwork three feet from the ground, and approached by steps on one side....

"Foiled in their attempts to enter our asylum, they next began to dig at its foundation; but the walls had been well laid, and were not so easily to be moved as they expected. They now fetched faggots, and from the circular construction of the building they were able to place them right in front of the doorway with impunity, there being no window or loop-hole in the place through which we could attack them, nor any means of so doing, without exposing ourselves to the whole mob at the entrance. In the centre of the temple there was an altar for the presentation of gifts to the presiding deity; his shrine, however, had not lately been enriched, or it had more recently been visited by his ministering priests, for there were no gifts upon it. There was, however, in a deep hole in the centre of the stone which constituted the altar, a hollow with a pint or two of water in it, which, although long since putrid, we baled out with our hands, and sucked down with great avidity. When the pile of faggots had reached the top of the doorway, or nearly so, they set them on fire, expecting to suffocate us; but a strong breeze kindly sent the great body of the smoke away from the interior of the temple. Fearing that the suffocating sultry atmosphere would be soon insupportable, I proposed to the men to sell their lives as dearly as possible; but we stood until the wood had sunk down into a pile of embers, and we began to hope that we might brave out their torture till night (apparently the only friend left us) would let us get out for food and attempted escape. But their next expedient compelled an evacuation; for they brought bags of gunpowder, and threw them upon the red-hot ashes. Delay would have been certain suffocation—so out we rushed. The burning wood terribly marred our bare feet, but it was no time to think of trifles. Jumping the parapet we were in the thick of the rabble in an instant; we fired a volley and ran a-muck with the bayonet."

One by one, making for the river, most of the poor fellows were shot down, some before reaching it, some while swimming for their lives. Most thankful was Mowbray Thomson now that a year or two before he had spent a guinea on learning to swim at the Holborn Baths. Only he, Lieutenant Delafosse, and two Irish privates escaped both the yelling crowd that thronged the bank, and not more cruel alligators that lurked here in the blood-stained water. Stripping themselves as they went, they swam on for two or three hours, the current helping to carry them away till the last of their pursuers dropped off; then they could venture to rest, up to their necks in water, plunging into the stream again at every sound. At length, utterly exhausted by fatigue and want of food, they saw nothing for it but to let themselves be dragged out by a band of natives, whose professions of friendliness they hardly credited, yet found them friends indeed. These four sole survivors of our force at Cawnpore were sheltered by a humane rajah till they could be safe in Havelock's ranks.

"When you got once more among your countrymen, and the whole terrible thing was over, what did you do first?" Thomson came to be asked, years afterwards; and his answer was, "Why, I went and reported myself as present and ready for duty."

Their less fortunate comrades in the boat, captured after such resistance as could be offered by its famished and fainting crew, had been taken back to Cawnpore. The men were ordered to be shot. One of the officers said a few prayers; they shook hands all round like Englishmen; the Sepoys fired, and finished the work with their swords. The women had to be dragged away from their husbands before this execution could be done. To the number of about thirty, including children, they were added to that band of captives in the Nana's hands, which presently became increased by another party of hapless fugitives from Futtehgurh, hoping here at last to find safety after an ordeal of their own, as we have already seen.

The fate of these prisoners is too well known. Some two hundred in all, they were confined for more than a fortnight within sight of the house where the Nana celebrated his doubtful triumph, under the coveted title of Peshwa, which he had now conferred upon himself. In want and woe, ill-fed, attended by "sweepers," that degraded caste whose touch is taken for pollution, they had to listen to the revelry of their tyrant's minions, and some were called on to grind corn for him, as if to bring home to them their slavish plight. Still, the worst was delayed. Probably the Nana had once meant to hold them as hostages. But as his affairs grew more disquieting, through the hate of rival pretenders, and the defeat of his troops before Havelock, perhaps enraged to fury perhaps rightly calculating that the British were urged on to such irresistible efforts by the hope of rescuing his captives, he resolved on a crime, for which the chief ladies of his own household, the widows of the adopted father to whom he owed everything, heathen as they were, are said to have called shame upon him, and threatened to commit suicide if he murdered any more of their sex.

The avenging army was now at hand, not to be frightened away by the roar of the idle salutes by which the Nana would fain have persuaded himself and others that he was indeed a mighty conqueror. Before going out to meet it on July 15th, he gave the order which has for ever loaded his name with infamy.[3] A few men, still suffered to live among the prisoners, were summoned forth. With them came the biggest of the boys, a lad of fourteen, fatally ambitious not to be counted among women and children. These were soon disposed of. Soon afterwards, a band of Sepoys were sent to fire into the house packed with its mob of helpless inmates; but the mutineers, who had done many a bloody deed, seem to have shrank from this. Half-a-dozen of them fired a few harmless shots, taking care to aim at the ceiling. Then were brought up five ruthless ruffians, fit for such work, two of them butchers by trade. By the quickly gathering gloom of Indian twilight, they entered the shambles, sword in hand; and soon shrieks and entreaties, dying down to groans through the darkness, told how these poor Christians came to an end of their sorrows. Proud, delicate English ladies, dusky Eurasians, sickly children, the night fell upon them all, never to see another sun.

One day more, and these unfortunates might have heard the guns of their advancing deliverer. After a succession of arduous combats, toiling through deep slush and sweltering air, Havelock had come within a few miles of Cawnpore, to find Nana Sahib waiting to dispute the passage with more than thrice his own numbers drawn up across the road. Very early in the morning, the British soldiers had been roused from their hungry bivouac in the open air. What their chief had to tell them was how he had heard of women and children still alive in Cawnpore; his clear voice broke into a sob as he cried, "With God's help, men, we shall save

[3] It is only fair to say that an attempt has been made so far to whitewash this hated name by representing the Nana as a dull, feeble tyrant, who, in this as in other actions, was the servant rather than the master of his ferocious soldiery.

them, or every man of us die in the attempt!" The men answered with three cheers, and needed no word of command to set out under the moonlight.

The sun rose upon the hottest day they had yet had to struggle through. A march of sixteen miles, that in itself was a trying day's work for India, brought them in sight of the enemy. Taken in flank by a careful manœuvre, the Sepoys were rolled up before the onrush of the Rossshire Buffs, and not now for the first or last time, had terror struck to their hearts by the fierce strains of the Highland bagpipe. Twice they rallied, but twice again our men drove them from their guns, to which English and Scots raced forward in eager rivalry. The blowing up of the Cawnpore magazine proclaimed a complete defeat. When night fell, the cowardly tyrant was flying amid his routed troops, and the weary Britons dropped to sleep on the ground they had won, cheered by hopes that the prize of the victory would be the lives of their country-folk.

It is said that on the night of this battle of Cawnpore, Havelock himself learned how he had come too late; but, in any case, his thousand men or less were not fit to be led a step further. Next day, when they entered the deserted city, their ranks began to be saddened by vague rumours of the tragedy they had toiled and bled to avert. But they could not realize the horror of it, till some Highlanders, prowling in search of drink or booty, came upon the house where their shoes plashed in blood and the floor was strewn with gory relics, strips of clothing, long locks of hair, babies' shoes and pinafores, torn leaves of paper, all soaked or stained with the same red tokens of what had been done within those walls. The trail of blood led them to a well in the court-yard, filled to the brim with mangled corpses—a sight from which brave men burst away in passionate tears and curses.

Over that gruesome spot now stands a richly-sculptured monument, where emblems of Christian faith and hope seem to speak peace to the souls of the victims buried beneath its silent marble. But who can wonder if, by such an open grave, our maddened soldiers then forgot all teachings of their creed, swearing wild oaths—oaths too well kept—to take vengeance on the heathen that thus made war with helpless women and children! Yet more worthy of our true greatness are the words of one who has eloquently chronicled the atrocities of Cawnpore, to draw from them the lesson, that upon their most deep-dyed scenes each Englishman should rather "breathe a silent petition for grace to do in his generation some small thing towards the conciliation of races estranged by a terrible memory"—alas! by more than one such memory.

Having reached Cawnpore too late, in spite of their utmost exertions, our small army had now before it the greater task of relieving Lucknow, believed to be in the utmost straits. But inevitable delays bridled their impatience. The Nana's troops were still in force not far off.

Even far in Havelock's rear, within a day's railway journey from Calcutta, there was an outbreak which had to be put down by the reinforcements hurrying up to his aid. Before we return to the siege of Delhi, a minor episode here should be related as one of the most gallant actions of the Mutiny, and yet no more than a characteristic sample of what Englishmen did in those days.

On July the 25th the Sepoys at Dinapore mutinied, and though stopped from doing much mischief there by the presence of European troops, managed to get safe away, as at Meerut, through the incapacity of a General unfit for command. Marching some twenty-five hundred strong to Arrah, a small station in the neighbourhood, they released the prisoners, plundered the treasury, and were joined by a mob of country-people, at the head of whom placed himself an influential and discontented nobleman named Koer Singh.

But here the few Europeans were prepared for the trial that now came upon them. The women and children being sent out of danger, a small house belonging to Mr. Wake, the magistrate, had been put in a state of defence, and stored with food and ammunition. It was an isolated building of one large room, used as a billiard-room, with cellars and arches below, and a flat roof protected by a parapet. Into this, the Englishmen, not twenty in number, betook themselves, with some fifty faithful Sikhs; and, almost all the former being sportsmen, if not soldiers, they kept up such a fire as taught the enemy to be very careful how they came too near their little stronghold.

The siege, however, was hotly pushed. A rain of balls fell, day and night, on the defences, behind which, strange to say, only a single man was seriously wounded, though the Sepoys fired from a wall not twenty yards off, and from the surrounding trees and the ditch of the compound. Two small cannon were brought to bear on the house, one from the roof of a bungalow which commanded it. An attempt had first been made to carry it by storm, but the defenders were so active at their loop-holes that the assailants did not care to try again. Other means failing, they set fire to a heap of red pepper on the windward side, hoping to smoke out the garrison. A not less serious annoyance was the stench of dead horses shot underneath the walls. But Wake and his brave band held out doggedly, and would not listen to any proposal for surrender.

Meanwhile, their friends at Dinapore were eager to make an effort for their relief. With some difficulty, the consent of the sluggish General was won, and over four hundred men steamed down the Ganges to land at the nearest point to Arrah. By bright moonlight they struck out over the flooded country. But the night-march was too hurried and careless. The relieving force, fired on from an ambush, fell into disastrous confusion, turned back, fighting their way into the boats, and got away with the loss of half their number. Yet, in that scene of panic and slaughter, some fugitives so distinguished themselves that two Victoria Crosses were earned on the retreat.

The besieged soon learned how their hopes of succour had been dashed down, and might well have given themselves up to despair. When the siege had lasted a week, it appeared not far from an end. The enemy were found to be running a mine against them. Water had luckily been dug down to under the house, but their food began to fail. Then, looking out on the morning of August 3, expecting perhaps to see the sun rise for the last time, to their astonishment they discovered no one to prevent them from sallying forth and capturing the sheep which had been feeding in the compound under their hungry eyes. The beleaguering Sepoys had unaccountably vanished.

Help was indeed at hand from another side. Vincent Eyre, a hero of the Afghan war, had been moving to their relief with not two hundred men and three guns. Though on the way he heard of the repulse of the Dinapore detachment, more than twice his own strength, he did not turn back. Making for an unfinished railway embankment as the best road to Arrah, he encountered Koer Singh's whole force of two or three thousand Sepoys and an unnumbered rabble, who crowded upon the little band, and must soon have swept them away by the mere weight of bullets. But the Englishmen charged into the thick of the crowd, and this time it was the enemy's turn to fly in dismay. Next day, the garrison of that billiard-room joyfully hailed the friends who had thus marvellously relieved them; and it is hard to say which had more right to be proud of their feat of arms. Koer Singh, beaten away from Arrah, nevertheless long held the field, and did his side good service by keeping the country in disorder, that helped to delay the advance of our troops to the fields on which they were so urgently needed.

Now has to be recorded a curious trait, very characteristic of Englishmen in India. While Havelock was waiting on the scene of that woeful massacre, till he should be able to advance, with such saddening memories fresh about them, with such deadly trials still before them, the officers kept up their spirits by organizing the "Cawnpore Autumn Race Meeting," which their pious General thought right to attend. The fawning or scowling natives, who now were fain at least to make some show of loyalty, must have thought the ways of Englishmen more unaccountable than ever.

# CHAPTER VI

## THE FALL OF DELHI

Three months the British army lay upon the Ridge running obliquely from the north-west angle of Delhi—that abrupt height two miles long, whose steep and broken front formed a natural fortification, strengthened by batteries and breast-works, among which the prominent points were at a house known as Hindoo Rao's, on the right of the position, and the Flagstaff Tower on the left, commanding the road to the Cashmere Gate of the city. The rear was protected by a canal that had to be vigilantly guarded, all the bridges broken down but one. The right flank was defended by strong works crowning that end of the ridge; the left rested on the straggling sandy bed of the Jumna, over-flooded by summer rains. The whole army, after the arrival of reinforcements in June, numbered not six thousand fighting men, a force barely sufficient to maintain such an extended line, even if a fifth of them had not been in hospital at once. Yet they not only held their own, but pushed their outposts far across the debatable plain between them and the city, seizing on the right an important point in the "Sammy House," the soldiers' slang name for a temple, and on their left recovering the grounds of Metcalf House, a splendid mansion that for weeks had been given up to the destructive hands of the rebels, who here spoiled one of the finest libraries in India.

As already pointed out, this was a complete reversal of the ordinary conditions of warfare. An army far inferior in numbers to its enemy attacked one corner of a city, six miles in circumference, open on all other sides to supplies of every kind, while the besiegers had much ado to keep up their own communications through a disturbed country, besides defending themselves against almost daily sallies of the nominally besieged. They were sorely tried by sickness, by deadly heat, then by wet weather that turned the river into an unwholesome swamp, and by a plague of flies swarming about the camp, with its abundant feast of filth and carrion. They were ill-provided with the means to carry on their urgent enterprise. Their lines were filled with spies among the native soldiers and camp-followers, who, at the best, only half wished them well. Everything they did, even what was designed in secret, seemed to be known presently at Delhi, so that the garrison were found prepared for all our movements; and thus the fresh plan of an assault in July had to be given up.

Even the irregular cavalry, judged for the most part more trusty than the foot Sepoys, came under strong suspicion when, by its connivance, as was believed, a band of the enemy's horse one day broke suddenly into the camp, causing a good deal of confusion, but were driven out before they could do much mischief. Other faithless servants were caught tampering with the artillery. But, in spite of all difficulties and discouragements, Lawrence's energetic support kept General Wilson sticking like a leech to his post, cautiously standing on the defensive, restoring the somewhat impaired discipline of his harassed ranks, and waiting till he should be strong enough to strike a decisive blow. The last thing to be thought of was retreat, for that signal of our discomfiture would have run like the Fiery Cross throughout Hindoostan.

We, too, had our spies, through whom we knew that those within the city were not without their troubles. There were quarrels between the devotees of the two hostile creeds, and between ambitious rivals for command. The old king, a puppet in the hands of his turbulent soldiery, might well sigh for peace. He wrote plaintive poetry describing his gilded woes; he talked of abdicating, of becoming a humble pilgrim, of giving himself up to the English; it is said that he even offered to admit our men at one of the gates, but this chance may have seemed too good to be trusted. The princes of his family began to think of making terms for themselves with the inevitable conquerors. The inhabitants were spoiled and oppressed by the Sepoys, vainly clamouring for the high pay they had been promised. Different regiments taunted one another's cowardice; but after one or two trials found themselves indisposed again to face our batteries without the walls.

When by the end of July, the fugitives from Cawnpore and elsewhere came dropping into Delhi with alarming accounts of Havelock's victories—of strange, terribly-plumed and kilted warriors, never seen before;[4] of mysterious Enfield rifle-balls that would kill at an unheard-of distance—the mutineers lost heart more and more, and in turn went on deserting from their new service; though there would still be a stream of reinforcements from those broken bodies which no longer cared to keep the open country.

To make up for want of real success, their leaders strove to inflame them by lying proclamations of victory and incitements to their superstitious zeal. The beginning of August brought in one of the great Mohamedan festivals, and this opportunity was taken to work up their enthusiasm for a fierce onslaught against our positions, from which, however, Sepoy and sowar once more rolled back disheartened, though one party had succeeded in pushing up almost to our left works, yelling out their religious watchwords, "Deen! Deen! Allah! Allah Achbar!" that could not silence the resolute British cheers. Another grand attack was attempted at the rear, but heaven seemed on our side rather than that of the Moslem fanatics, for an opportune deluge of rain swelled the canal to a torrent and swept away their attempts at bridging it. Every effort on their part was foiled, while to the right we made progress in mastering the Kissengunge suburb, and on the left pushed forward half-a-mile from Metcalf House to seize the enemy's guns at a building called Ludlow Castle, formerly the Commissioner's residence, which lay almost under the city walls.

[4] When the Highlanders first appeared in India, a report is said to have spread among the natives that English men running short, we had sent our women into the field; but the prowess of the new warriors soon corrected that misapprehension.

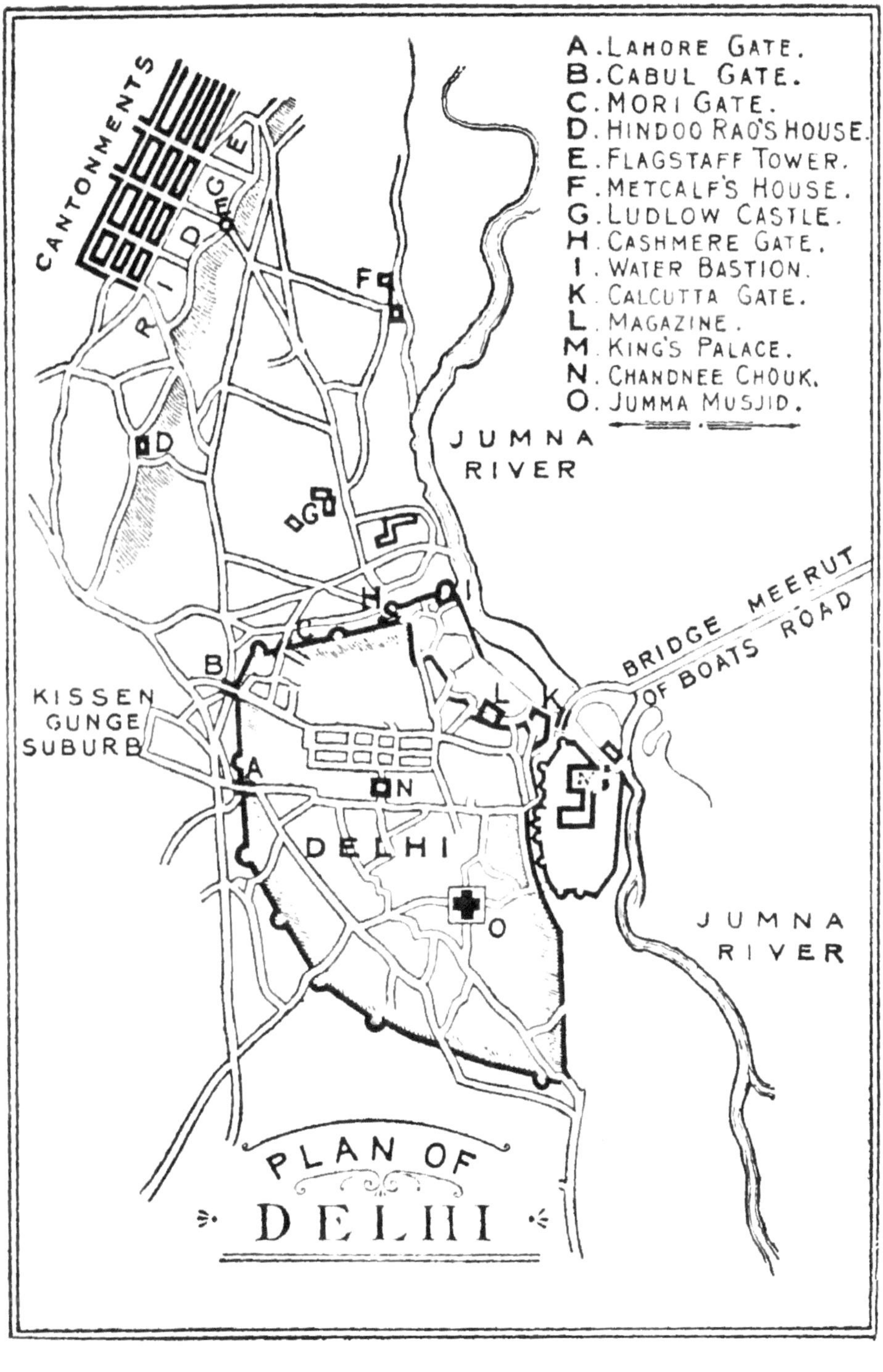


Plan of Delhi.

On August 7 a powder-magazine blew up on the further side of Delhi, killing hundreds of men. This disaster was the more appalling to the rebels when they learned that a heavy siege-train was advancing to remount our feeble batteries. Six thousand men sallied forth, making a circuit far to our rear in hope to cut off the train. But their movements had been watched. They were followed and defeated with heavy loss, the first exploit of Nicholson, who arrived with his Punjaub column about the middle of August to put new vigour into the attack. This officer, still young for command, had years before won a reputation far beyond his age; and now, as soon as he appeared on the scene of action, seems to have made himself felt as its moving spirit, so much so, that in the story of it, his eager vehemence stands out as too much throwing into the shade the caution supplied by General Wilson, unduly disparaged by Nicholson' admirers. We had need at once here of prudence and of valour in the highest degree.

At length the slow siege-train, drawn by a hundred elephants, after so long, literally, sticking in the mud, came up on September 3rd. On the Ridge all was ready for it. Works sprang up like mushrooms, and in a few days forty heavy guns began playing upon the northern face of the city. Batteries were pushed forward to almost within musket-shot; then, day by day, the massive walls and bastions were seen crashing into ruins at several points. Formidable as they were in older warfare, they did not resist modern artillery so well as less pretentious earthworks might have done.

By the 13th two breaches seemed practicable. That night four young engineer officers, with a few riflemen, stole up through the jungle to the Cashmere Bastion, passing behind the enemy's skirmishers. They dropped into the ditch unseen, and had almost mounted the broken wall when discovered by its sentries, whose random shots whizzed about them as they ran back to report that a way was open for the stormers.

The assault was at once ordered for three o'clock of that morning, September 14. Under cover of darkness, the troops eagerly advanced in four columns, the first, led by Nicholson, against the breach near the Cashmere Bastion; the second directed upon another breach at the Water Bastion; the third to storm the Cashmere Gate, after it had been blown up; while the fourth, far to the right, should attack the Lahore Gate, through the Kissengunge suburb.

A reserve followed the first three columns, ready to follow up their success; and the 60th Rifles, scattered through wooded ground in front, were to keep down the fire of the enemy from the walls. The cavalry and horse artillery, under Sir Hope Grant, held themselves ready for repulsing any sortie to which our ill-guarded camp would now lie exposed.

The whole army numbered under nine thousand men, rather more than a third of them English soldiers. There was a contingent of native allies from Cashmere, who did not give much assistance when it came to fighting. Our Punjaubee auxiliaries, however, proved more serviceable, burning for the humiliation and spoil of this Moslem Sanctuary, against which the Sikhs bore an old religious grudge.

Unfortunately there came about some delay, and daylight had broken before the three left columns were ready to advance from Ludlow Castle, under a tremendous artillery fire from both sides. The advantage of a surprise was thus lost. Suddenly our guns fell silent, a bugle rang out, and forth dashed the stormers upon the walls manned to receive them with fire and steel. Nicholson's column found that something had been done to repair the breach; and so thick was the hail of bullets to which they stood exposed in the open, that for several minutes they could not even gain the ditch, man after man being struck down in placing the ladders. But, once across that difficulty, they scrambled up the breach, where the raging and cursing rebels hurled its fragments down upon them, but, for all their shouts of defiance, did not await a struggle hand to hand. They fled before the onset, and our men poured in through the undefended gap.

The same success, and the same losses, attended the second column, making good its entry at the Water Bastion. A way for the third had been opened by a resounding deed of heroism, which struck popular imagination as the chief feature of this daring assault. The Cashmere Gate, that from first to last plays such a part in the story of Delhi, must be blown up to give the assailants passage into the bastion from which it faces sideways. Lieutenants Home and Salkeld, of the Engineers, with three sergeants and a bugler, formed the forlorn hope that dashed up to the gate, each loaded with 25 lbs. of powder in a bag. The enemy were so amazed at this audacity that for a moment they offered no opposition as the gallant fellows sped across the shattered drawbridge, and began to lay their bags against the heavy wood-work of the inner gate. But then from the wicket and from the top of the gateway they found themselves fired at point-blank, resolutely completing their task. Home, after his bag was placed, had the luck to jump into the ditch unhurt. Salkeld was shot in two places, but handed the portfire to a sergeant, who fell dead. The next man lighted the fuse at the cost of a mortal wound; and the third sergeant did not save himself till he saw the train well alight. A bugle-note calling forward the stormers was drowned in the roar of a terrific explosion, as the 52nd, held in leash for this signal, eagerly sprang on to pour through the smoking ruins. Thus all three columns, about the same time, had lodged themselves within the defences.

While the third column pushed forward into the heart of the city, and the supporting parties moved up to occupy the points taken, the rest of the assailants turned to their right by a road which ran at the back of the ramparts, clearing them as they went, and mastering the Mori and Cabul Gates from behind; then tried to make their way towards the Lahore Gate where they hoped to join hands with the fourth column. But this, repulsed by a slaughterous fire and its leader wounded, had alone failed in the errand assigned to it. Here, too, the routed Sepoys rallied within their walls, and brought guns to bear down a narrow lane in which the progress of Nicholson's column was fatally arrested. The young General himself, the foremost hero of that day, fell shot through the body while cheering on his men, and with his life-blood ebbed for a time the tide of victory that had swept him on hitherto without a check. He was carried away to die in the camp, yet not till he knew Delhi to be fully won. His force had to fall back to the Cabul Gate, and for the meanwhile stand upon the defensive.

The third column, under Colonel Campbell, had met less opposition in penetrating straight into the city, guided by Sir Thomas Metcalf, who, though a civilian, had all along made himself most useful by his thorough knowledge of the localities. Charging through lanes, bazaars, and open spaces, they crossed the palace gardens, forced a passage over the Chandnee Chouk, "Silver Street," the main commercial thoroughfare of Delhi, and threaded their way by narrow winding streets right up to the Jumma Musjid, or Great Mosque, whose gigantic steps, colonnades and cupolas tower so majestically over the centre of the Mogul's capital. But here they were brought to a stand before solid walls and gates, having neither guns nor powder-bags to break their way further, while from the buildings around the enemy poured destruction into the chafing ranks. They had to withdraw to an enclosure, which was held for an hour and a half under hot fire; and when Colonel Campbell learned how the other column could not get beyond the Cabul Gate to support him, he saw nothing for it but to retire upon the ruined English Church near the Cashmere Gate, as did a party he had detached to occupy the police office.

The result of the first day's fighting, then, was that, with a dear loss of nearly twelve hundred killed and wounded, our soldiers had ensconced themselves along the north side of the walls, where, throwing up hasty defences, they prepared to be in turn attacked by a host of still resolute warriors.

England's glory was now mingled with England's shame. The crafty foe, knowing our men's besetting sin, would appear to have purposely strewn the emptied streets with bottles of wine, beer, and spirits, the most effectual weapons they could have used, for on them the parched Saxons fell with such greedy thirst that by next morning a large part of the army was, in plain English, helplessly drunk, and it seemed hopeless to attempt any progress that day. Our Sikh and Goorkha auxiliaries, for their part, thought less of fighting than of securing the long-expected loot of a city so famed for riches. Had the enemy been more active, he could have taken such an opportunity of turning victory into ruin by a resolute diversion in the assailants' rear, two or three miles as they now were from their slightly guarded camp and base of supplies. General Wilson, trembling to think that even yet he might have to make a disastrous retreat, ordered all liquor found to be destroyed, and took steps to restrain the licence of plundering, which is always a temptation to disorder for a storming army as well as a cruel terror for the inhabitants.

Thanks to his measures, Wednesday the 16th found the force more fit to follow up its success, and that day ended with a considerable advance in regaining the city, point after point, against a resistance growing daily feebler. The arsenal was captured with a great number of guns. Next day again, still further progress was made; then up to the end of the week the assailants went on winning their way, street by street, to the Royal Palace and the Great Mosque. These spacious edifices, as well as the long-contested Lahore Gate, were easily carried on Sunday, the 20th, the mass of the rebels having fled by night through the gates beyond, leaving desolate streets, where the remnant of panic-stricken inhabitants durst hardly show their faces.

Tomb of Humayoon, Delhi.

Ruins of old Delhi.

Everywhere now prevailed ruin and silence over the captured city. For our soldiers, that Sunday afternoon might at length be a time of rest, their hard and bloody week's work done when the British flag flew once more over the palace of the Grand Mogul, and the Queen's health was triumphantly drunk upon his deserted throne. A wild riot of pillage and destruction ran through the famous halls, on which is inscribed what must have now read such a mockery: "If on earth there be a Paradise, it is here!" To this monument of Oriental splendour, the last monarch of his race was soon brought a humble captive.

The old king, who cuts such a pitiful figure throughout those tragic scenes, refusing to follow the flying troops, with his wife and family had taken sanctuary in one of the vast lordly tombs that rise over the buried ruins of old Delhi, stretching for leagues beyond the present limits of the city. Time-serving informers hastened to betray his refuge to one who had neither fear of peril nor respect for misfortune. Hodson of Hodson's Horse, a name often prominent in this history, an old Rugby boy of the Tom Brown days, was a man as to whose true character the strangest differences of opinion existed even among those who knew him best; but no one ever doubted his readiness when any stroke of daring was to be done. The city scarcely mastered, he offered to go out and seize the king, to which General Wilson consented on the unwelcome condition that his life should be spared.

With fifty of his irregular troopers, Hodson galloped off to the tomb, an enormous mausoleum of red stone, inlaid with marble and surmounted by a marble dome, its square court-yard enclosed in lofty battlemented walls with towers and gateways, forming a veritable fortress, which had indeed, in former days, served as a citadel of refuge. That Sunday afternoon the sacred enclosure swarmed with an excited multitude, among whom Hodson and his men stood for two hours, awaiting an answer to their summons for the king's surrender. Cowering in a dimly-lit cell within, the unhappy old man was long in making up his mind; but finally, yielding to the terrified or traitorous councils of those around him, he came forth with his favourite wife and youngest son, and gave up his arms, asking from the Englishman's own lips a renewal of the promise that their lives should be spared. In palanquins they were slowly carried back to his gorgeous palace, where the descendant of the Moguls found himself now a prisoner, treated with contempt, and indebted for his life to the promise of an English officer—a promise openly regretted by some in the then temper of the conquerors.

A more doubtful deed of prowess was to make Hodson doubly notorious. Learning that two of the king's sons and a grandson were still lurking in that tomb of their ancestors, he went out again next day with a hundred troopers, and demanded their unconditional surrender. Again the crowd stood cowed before his haughty courage. Again the fugitives spent time in useless parley, while, surrounded by thousands of sullen natives, Hodson bore himself as if he had an army at his back. At length the princes, overcome by the determination of this masterful Briton, came forth from their retreat, and gave themselves up to his mercy. They were placed in a cart, and taken towards the city under a small guard, Hodson remaining behind for an hour or two to see the crowd give up its arms, as they actually did at his command; then he galloped after the captives, and overtook them not far from the walls of Delhi.

Thus far all had gone well; but now came the dark feature of the story that has given rise to so much debate. Hodson's account is that the mob, which he had hitherto treated with such cool contempt, became threatening when he had almost reached the Lahore Gate, causing a fear that the prisoners might even yet be rescued. His accusers assert that he let himself be overcome by the lust for vengeful slaughter which then possessed too many a British heart. Riding up to the cart, he ordered the princes to dismount and strip. Then, in a loud voice proclaiming them the murderers of English women and children, with his own hand he shot all three dead. The naked bodies, thus slain without trial or deliberation, were exposed to public view in the Chandnee Chouk, as stern warning of what it was to rouse the old Adam in English nature.

Wilson's army might now draw a deep breath of relief after successfully performing such a critical operation, the results of which should be quickly and widely felt. Like a surgeon's lancet, it had at last been able to prick the festering sore that was the chief head of far-spread inflammation. The fall of the Mogul's capital was a signal for rebellion to hide its head elsewhere. Doubtful friends, wavering allies, were confirmed, as our open enemies were dismayed, by the tidings which let India's dusky millions know how British might had prevailed against the proudest defiance.

At the seat of war, indeed, this good effect was not at once so apparent as might have been expected; the result being rather to let loose thousands of desperate Sepoys for roving mischief, while even hitherto inactive mutineers now rushed into the field as if urged by resentful fury. But immediate and most welcome was the relief in the Punjaub, where our power seemed strained to breaking-point by the tension of delay in an enterprise for which almost all its trustworthy troops had been drawn away, leaving the country at the mercy of any sudden rising, such as did take place at two or three points among the agitated population. But the fear of that danger was lost in the good news from Delhi, as soon as it could be trusted.

Not the least trouble of our people in those days was the want of certain news, to let them know how it stood with their cause amid the blinding waves of rebellion. The mails were stopped or passed irregularly. Native messengers could not be depended upon, magnifying the danger through terror, or dissembling it through ill-will; truth is always a rare commodity in India. Many a tiny letter went and came rolled in an inch of quill sewed away in the bearer's dress, or carried in his mouth to be swallowed in an instant, for, if detected, he was like to be severely punished. Officers were fain to correspond with each other by microscopic missives written in Greek characters, a remnant of scholarship thus turned to account against the case of their falling into hostile hands. The natives, for their part, though often ill-served by their own ignorance and proneness to exaggeration, were marvellously quick to catch the rumours of our misfortunes, which spread from mouth to mouth as by some invisible telegraph. They did not prove always so ready to appreciate the signs of a coming restoration of our supremacy, once the tide had turned. All over India the eyes of white men and black had been fixed eagerly on Delhi; then while English hearts had become more than once vainly exalted by false rumours of its fall, when this did take place at length, the population, even of the surrounding country, showed themselves slow to believe in the catastrophe.

General Wilson at once followed up his success by sending out a column under Colonel Greathed to pursue the Sepoys who were making for Oudh. All went smoothly with this expedition, till Greathed had letters urgently begging him to turn aside for the relief of Agra, believed to be threatened by the advance of another army of mutineers from Central India. By forced marches the column made for Agra, where it arrived on the morning of October 10, and was received with great jubilation by the crowd pent up within the walls. But to the end it seemed as if the drama enacted on that gorgeous scene was destined to have tragi-comic features. The Agra people, under the mistaken idea that their enemies had fallen back, gave themselves to welcoming their friends, when mutual congratulations were rudely interrupted by the arrival, after all, of the Sepoys, who had almost got into the place without being observed. Sir George Campbell, so well-known both as an Indian official and as a member of Parliament, describes the scene of amazement and confusion that followed. He was at breakfast with a friend who had ventured to re-occupy his house beyond the walls, when a sound of firing was heard, at first taken for a salute, but soon suggesting something more serious. Sir George got out his horse, borrowed a revolver, and galloped down to the parade, on which he found round shot hopping about like cricket-balls.

"It turned out that the enemy had completely surprised us. Instead of retreating, they had that morning marched straight down the metalled high-road—not merely a surprise party, but the whole force, bag and baggage, with all their material and many guns, including some exceedingly large ones; but no one took the least notice of them. There was a highly-organized Intelligence Department at Agra, who got unlimited news, true and false, but on this occasion no one brought any news at all. The only circumstance to favour the advance was that the high millet crops were on the ground, some of them ten or twelve feet high, and so the force marching down the road was not so visible as it would have been at another time. They reached the point where the road crossed the parade-ground quite unobserved. They probably had some scouts, and discovering our troops there, arranged themselves and got their guns in position before they announced themselves to us. The first attack was made by a few fanatics, who rushed in and cut down two or three of our men, but were not numerous enough to do material harm. If the enemy's real forces had made a rush in the same way, when no one expected them, there is no saying what might have happened; but, fortunately, as natives generally do, they believed in and stuck to their great guns, and instead of charging in, they opened that heavy fire which had disturbed us at breakfast."

The Sepoys, in fact, had also been surprised, not knowing that a European force had reached Agra before them. Our soldiers at once got under arms; then a battery of artillery, the 9th Lancers, and a regiment of Sikhs were first to arrive on the ground. The rest came up before long, at first in some doubt as to who was friend or foe. A charge of the enemy's cavalry had almost been taken for our own people running away. Then these troopers, broken by a charge of the Lancers, "were galloping about the parade and our men firing at them as if it were a kind of big battue." Some of the routed sowars got near enough to the lines to cause a general panic there; and the way to the scene of action was blocked by men wildly galloping back for the fort, some of them, it is said, on artillery horses which they had stolen. "Everybody was riding over everybody else."

Once the confusion got straightened out, however, the hardened Delhi troops were not long in repelling this unexpected attack. A tumbrel blew up among the Sepoys, and that seemed to be a sign of disheartenment for them. They began to give way, making a stand here and there, but soon fled in complete rout, leaving their baggage and guns to the victors, who chased them for several miles.

Sir George Campbell, though a civilian, has to boast of more than one amusing exploit on this battle-field. In the heat of pursuit, his horse ran away with him, and, much against his will, carried him right towards a band of Sepoys hurrying off a train of guns. All he could do was to wave his sword and shout, partly to bring up assistance, and partly in the hope of frightening the enemy. It is said that the battle of Alma was perhaps decided by the accident of Lord Raglan rashly straying right within the Russian position, when the enemy, seeing an English general officer and his staff among them, took it for granted that all must be lost. So it was with these Sepoys, who forthwith ran away, leaving three guns, which Sir George could claim to have captured by his single arm, but did not know what to do with them. It occurred to him to shoot the leading bullock of each gun-team, to prevent the rest getting away, while he went to seek for assistance; then he found that his borrowed pistol would not go off. In the end, the three guns were brought back to Agra in triumph, and probably form part of the show of obsolete artillery and ammunition exhibited to travellers within the walls of its vast fortress.

"One more adventure I had which somewhat detracted from my triumph with the guns. I overtook an armed rebel, not a Sepoy, but a native matchlock-man; he threw away his gun, but I saw that he had still a large powder-horn and an old-fashioned pistol in his belt; my blood was up, and I dealt him a mighty stroke with my sword, expecting to cut him almost in two, but my swordsmanship was not perfect; he did not fall dead as I expected; on the contrary, he took off his turban, and presenting his bare head to me, pointed to a small scratch and said, 'There, Sahib, evidently God did not intend you to kill me, so you may as well let me off now.' I felt very small; evidently he had the best of the argument. But he was of a forgiving disposition, and relieved my embarrassment by cheerful conversation, while he professed, as natives do, that he would serve me for the rest of his life. I made him throw away any arms he still had, safe-conducted him to the nearest field, and we parted excellent friends; but I did not feel that I had come very gloriously out of it. I have never since attempted to use a sword as an offensive weapon, nor, I think I may say, attempted to take the life of any fellow-creature."

Such amusing episodes come welcome in this grimly tragic story. But, indeed, it is remarkable to note how our countrymen, at the worst, never quite lost their sense of humour. Some singular proofs of Mark Tapleyish spirit, under depressing circumstances, are supplied by Mr. J.W. Sherer's narrative, incorporated in Colonel Maude's recent *Memoirs of the Mutiny*. Mr. Sherer, like Edwards, had to run from his post, and came near to sharing the same woes, but while the latter's book might be signed *Il Penseroso*, the other is all *L'Allegro*. Looking over Indian papers of that day, among the most dismaying news and the most painful rumours, one finds squibs in bad verse and rough jokes, not always in the best taste, directed against officers who seemed wanting in courage, or stations where the community had given way to ludicrous panic without sufficient cause. Some unintended absurdities appear, also, due no doubt to native compositors or to extraordinary haste, as when one newspaper declares that a certain regiment has "covered itself with *immoral* glory!"

On the whole, however, editors were more disposed to be bloodthirsty than facetious. After forty years have put us in a position to look more calmly on that welter of hate and dread, one reads with a smile how fiercely the men of pen and ink called out for prompt action, for rapid movements, for ruthless severities—why was not Delhi taken at once?—why were reinforcements not hurried up to this point or that?—what was such and such an officer about that he did not overcome all resistance as easily as it could be done on paper? The time was now at hand, when these remonstrances could be made with less unreason. The rebellion had been fairly got under with the fall of Delhi; and the rest would mainly be a matter of patience and vigilance, though at one point the flames still glowed in perilous conflagration.

# CHAPTER VII

## THE DEFENCE OF LUCKNOW

The focus of the insurrection was now at Lucknow, where ever since the end of June the Residency defences had been besieged by the rebels of Oudh, and thus most serviceably kept engaged a host of fighters, who might else have marched to turn the wavering scale at Delhi. Apart from its practical result, the gallantry displayed, both by the much-tried garrison and by two armies which successfully broke through to their aid, has marked this defence as one of the principal scenes of the Indian Mutiny and one of the most stirring episodes in modern history. Some of the closing scenes of the war, also, long after the Residency had been gloriously abandoned, came to be enacted round the same spot, for ever sacred to English valour.

There is no Englishman's heart but must thrill to behold those patches of blackened and riddled ruin, half-hidden among gorgeous Eastern flowers, where idle cannon stand now as trophies by the battered walls, and brown-limbed gardeners water the smooth turf-lawns once drenched with so brave blood. Set in a beautiful garden, the remnants of the Residency buildings are preserved no less reverently than the tombs and monuments of their defenders, over which rises the flowery mound that bears aloft a white cross sacred to the memory of the Christian dead, famous and nameless, lying side by side around. Pillars and tablets carefully record the situation of this and that post, house, or battery, some hardly traceable now, some mere shells, or no more than names; but the ground has been so much changed by the clearing away of *débris* and the demolition of adjacent structures, that it is difficult for us to realize the scene, some of the chief actors in which, years afterwards, found themselves not quite clear as to all its original features. A model, however, preserved in the Lucknow Museum, presents the localities restored as far as possible to their original state, according to the best authorities, giving us some idea of what this frail fortress was, and exciting our amazement that it held out for a single day.[5]

[5] The author has gone over the ground, noting its features on the spot; but for refreshing his memory and making all the positions clear, he has to acknowledge his obligation especially to the pictures and plans in General McLeod Innes' *Lucknow and Oude in the Mutiny*.

City of Lucknow.

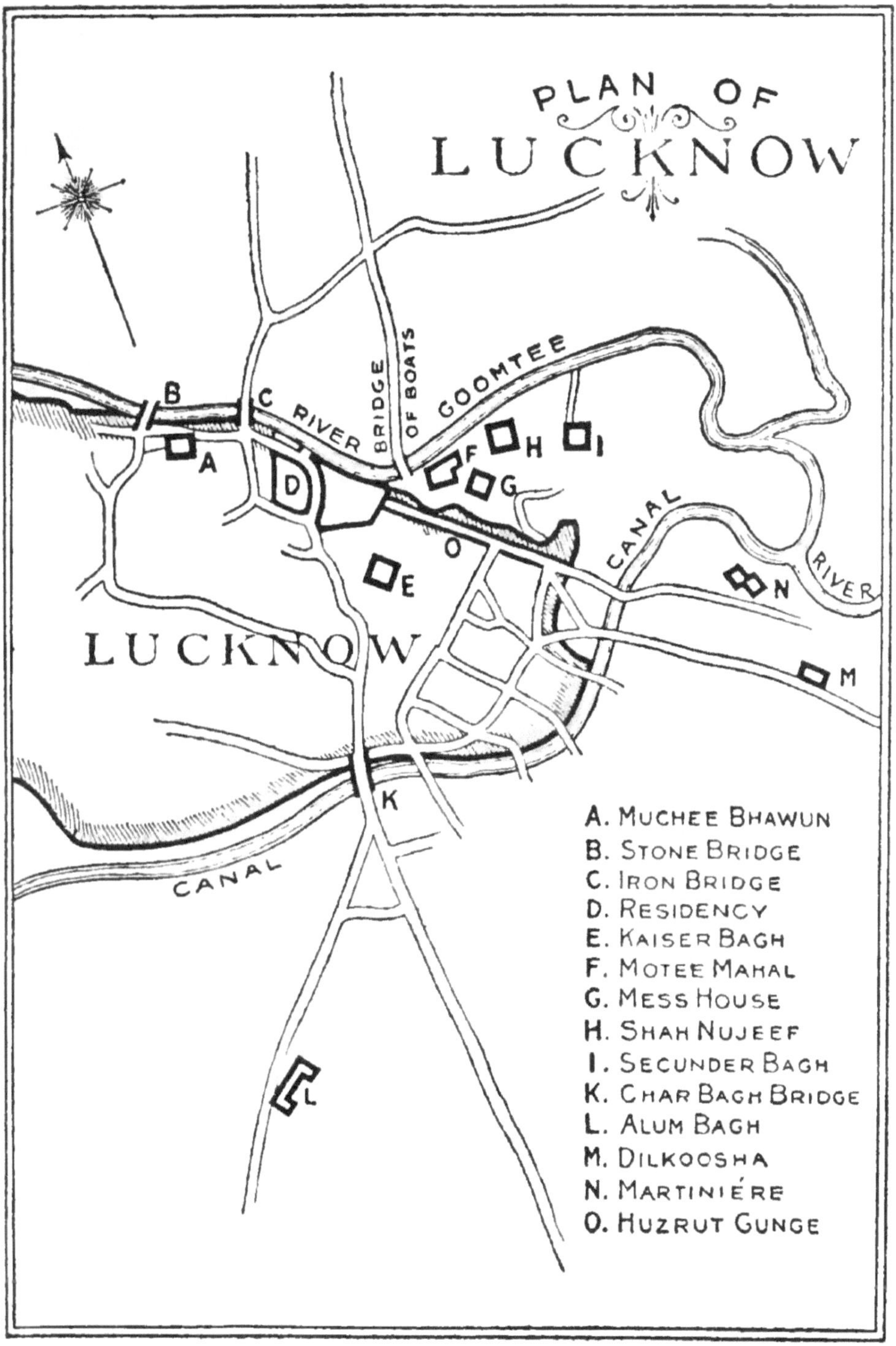


Plan of Lucknow.

We must not, then, imagine a citadel enclosed by solid walls like those of Delhi or the palatial fort at Agra, but a group of buildings widely scattered round the tower of the Residency, the outer ones turned each into a defensive work, with its own separate garrison, the gaps between filled up as means or accidents of situation best allowed. Mud walls, banks, hedges, ditches, lanes, trees, palisades and barricades, were all put to use for these irregular and extemporary fortifications, composed among other materials of carriages, carts, boxes, valuable furniture, and even a priceless library that went to stop bullets. It would take too long to give a full description of all the points made memorable by this siege, such as the Bailey Guard Gate, the Cawnpore Battery, the Sikh Square, Gubbins' House, the Church Post, the Redan, which formed the most salient features of the circle marked out for defence. The hastily thrown-up bastions were not finished when that rout of Chinhut made them so needful. A bolder enemy might have carried the lines at once with a rush. The half-ruined buildings outside gave the assailants cover within pistol-shot of the besieged; while indeed the latter were thus to a large extent shielded against artillery fire, as had been Lawrence's design in not completing his work of destruction here. Some of the rebel batteries played upon the works at a range of from fifty to a hundred yards. On one side, only a dozen yards of roadway separated the fighters; and from behind their palisades the loyal Sepoys could often exchange abuse, as well as shots, with the mutineers, who would steal up at night, tempting them to desert, as many did in the course of the siege, yet not so many as might have been expected under such trying circumstances.

This entrenchment was occupied by nearly a thousand soldiers, civilians, clerks, traders, or travellers turned by necessity into fighting-men, with a rather less number of staunch Sepoys, as well as about five hundred women and children, shuddering at the peril of a fate so fearful that English ladies kept poison ready for suicide in case of the worst, and loving husbands promised to shoot their wives dead, rather than let them fall alive into hands freshly blood-stained from the horrors of Cawnpore. As there a girls' school were among the victims, so at Lucknow the motley garrison included the boys of the Martinière College, whose experiences have been already mentioned. In all, counting some hundreds of native servants, not far short of three thousand persons must have been crowded within an irregular enclosure about a mile round, where on that disastrous last day of June the enemy's bullets began to fly across a scene of dismay and confusion—men hardly yet knowing their places or their duties; women wild with fear; bullocks, deserted by their attendants, wandering stupidly about in search of food; horses, maddened by thirst, kicking and biting one another, in the torment which no one had time to relieve. The siege had come to find these people too little prepared for its trials, or for the length to which it was protracted. Some thought they might have to hold out a fortnight. Few guessed that their ordeal would endure nearly five months.

When, on June 30th, the city fell into the hands of the rebels, we still occupied another position not far from the Residency, the old fortress of Muchee Bhawun, which, though more imposing in appearance, was not fit to resist artillery, nor, after the losses of Chinhut, were there men enough to defend both points. On the second day of the siege, therefore, Colonel Palmer, commanding here, was ordered by semaphore signals from the Residency tower, to bring his force into the other entrenchment, spiking the guns, and blowing up what ammunition he could not carry away. At midnight he marched silently through the city, without attracting any notice from the enemy, who were perhaps too busy plundering elsewhere. They had hardly joined their comrades, when a terrific explosion announced the destruction of the Muchee Bhawun, blown up by a train set to go off in half-an-hour. One soldier had been accidentally left behind, who, strange to say, escaped unhurt from the explosion, and next morning walked coolly into the Residency, meeting no one to stop him, perhaps because he was quite naked, and the people took him for a madman or a holy man!

It was sad news that awaited Colonel Palmer. His daughter, while sitting in an upper room of the Residency, had been wounded by a shell, one of the first among many victims. She died in a few days, by which time the besieged had to mourn a greater loss. The Residency building, elevated above the rest, was soon seen to be a prominent mark for the enemy's fire, and on the first day, after a shell had burst harmlessly in his own room, Lawrence was begged to move into less dangerous quarters. With characteristic carelessness of self, he put off doing so; then next morning, July 2, was mortally wounded while lying on his bed. Two days later he died, visited by many weeping friends, of whom he took leave in the spirit of an earnest Christian. Well known is the epitaph which, amid the din of shot and shell, he dictated for his grave: *"Here lies Henry Lawrence, who tried to do his duty. May the Lord have mercy on his soul!"* He nominated Major Banks as his successor in the Commissionership and Brigadier Inglis to command the troops. The latter had his wife with him throughout all, to whose recently published reminiscences we owe one of the most interesting narratives of the siege.

Gloom fell upon the garrison when they came to learn this heavy loss. Every man had so much to do at his own post, that he hardly knew what went on a few hundred yards off, and some days seem to have passed before it leaked out to all how their leader had been buried "darkly at dead of night," in the same pit with less distinguished dead. A common grave had to be dug each night, the churchyard being exposed to fire. Every day now had its tale of deaths, soon from fifteen to twenty, once the enemy had got the range and given up wild firing at random—an average which grew smaller as the besieged were taught to be more cautious in exposing themselves. Six weeks passed before the diary of the chaplain's wife can record, for once, a day without a single funeral. Death was busy everywhere in various forms. Men were more than once buried beneath the ruins of houses crushed by the storm of shot. Delicate women panted for air in crowded cellars, and sickened amid the pestilential stenches that beset every corner of the entrenchment, or despairingly saw their children pine away for want of proper nourishment. The poor sufferers in hospital would sometimes be wounded afresh or killed outright by balls crashing among them. An amputation was almost certain death in that congregation of gangrened sufferers, increased hour by hour. There were daily duties to be done always at the peril of men's lives, and spots where no one could show himself without the risk of drawing fire. "Many a poor fellow was shot, who was too proud to run past places where bullets danced on the walls like a handful of peas in a fry-pan." One building, called "Johannes' House," overlooking the defences as it did, was long a thorn in the side of the besieged, from the top of which a negro eunuch, whom they nicknamed "Bob the Nailer," was believed to have shot down dozens of them by the unerring aim of a double-barrelled rifle that gave him such grim celebrity.

The native servants soon began to desert, adding to the troubles of masters whose pride and practice had been to do nothing that could be helped for themselves. Then the younger Martinière boys were told off to take their place in the cramped households, set to perform the menial services looked upon as belonging to the lowest caste. They attended the sick, too, and were of especial use in defending them against an Egyptian plague of flies which assailed the entrenchment, as well as in pulling punkahs to cool fevered brows. All these school-boys, whose terrible holidays began so unseasonably, took their turns in washing, grinding corn, bringing wood and water, besides general fetching and carrying at various posts, while some dozen of the oldest stood guard, musket in hand, or helped to work the signals on the tower—a service of no small danger, as the movements of the semaphore drew a hot fire; and, what with the clumsiness of the apparatus and the cutting of the ropes by shot, it took three hours to convey the order for evacuation of the Muchee Bhawun.

Though their post seems to have been an exposed one, just opposite Johannes' House, where that black marksman stationed himself, and where the enemy were literally just across the street, the school-boys had throughout only two of their number wounded, while two died of disease. Mr. Hilton, whose narrative has been already quoted, can tell of more than one narrow escape, once when a spent cannon-ball passed between his legs; again when a fragment of shell smashed the cooking pot from which he was about to draw his ration; and another time he was assisting to work the semaphore on the roof, when a shell burst so near as to disgust him with that duty. He did manage to get hurt in a singular manner. A badly-aimed shell from one of their own batteries fell into the court-yard where he was sitting, and in the wild stampede which ensued he stumbled over his sister and cut his knee on a sharp stone. This wound ought to have healed in a few days, but constant hardship had thrown him into such a bad state of health, that it festered and kept him in pain for more than two months, under the terrible warning that his leg might have to be amputated if he did not take care of it.

Before this accident he had entered into his duties as a soldier with rather more zeal than discretion. The boys trusted with arms, used, it seems, to take ten or twenty rounds to the top of the house, and fire through the loop-holes at whatever seemed a fair target. Fed on stews of tough beef and coarse *chupatties*, the hand-cakes of the country, their mouths watered at the sight of pumpkins and other vegetables growing in Johannes' garden, just beyond the line of their defences, so near yet so far out of reach; for the Sepoy marksmen were always on the watch to shoot any one who exposed himself here. Seeing they could not get these gourds for themselves, the lads found amusement in shooting at them to spoil them at least for the enemy. But this sport was soon interfered with. One boy having been wounded by a rebel lurking in the sheds opposite, Hilton and a comrade, named Luffman, went up to the roof to get a shot at the fellow. While they were firing from a loop-hole protected by a basket full of rubbish, another boy came out to join them with a fresh supply of ammunition; then their attention being for a moment diverted to him, the Sepoy over the way saw his chance for an aim. His bullet struck Luffman's musket, glanced along the barrel, and lodged in the lad's left shoulder. This accident drew on the young marksmen a severe reprimand from the Principal, and their supplies of ammunition for promiscuous shooting were henceforth cut off.

Mr. Hilton makes no complaint on his own account; but Mr. Rees, an ex-master of the Martinière, who has also given us an account of the siege, says that the boys were rather put upon in his opinion. He describes them as going about "more filthy than others, and apparently more neglected and hungry." Up till the end of June they had been able to draw supplies of food and clean clothes from the college. Now they were reduced to what they had on their backs, a serious trial in the Indian climate, and had to do their washing for themselves as best they could. The Martinière was in the hands of the mutineers, who had wreaked their wrath by digging up poor General Martin's tomb and scattering his bones.

One honourable charge these youngsters had. There was a store of wines and spirits in the garrison, which some of the soldiers broke into, and were once found helplessly drunk when called to arms on a sudden alarm. After that, the liquor was guarded in the Martinière post, till it could be disposed of so as to do least mischief.

The women, who in private houses or in the underground vaults of the Residency were kept out of danger as well as possible, had their share of toils, to which some would be little used. Many found enough to do in looking after their own ailing families. Others distinguished themselves by zeal in tending the sick and wounded. The wonder is that the diseases which had broken out from the first did not sweep off the whole community, pent up in such unwholesome confinement. Fortunately, in the course of a few days, a heavy shower of rain fell to wash away the filth that was poisoning them. This was the opening of the rainy season, on the whole welcome, yet not an unmixed blessing. The climate of India runs always to extremes; so glare and dust were exchanged only for the enervation of a perpetual vapour-bath.

In heat and wet, by night and day, every able-bodied man must take weary spells of watching and working, and at all hours be ready to run to his post on the first sign of danger. Nearly fifty guns had to be served. Officers and men, civilians and soldiers, black and white, laboured side by side, a tool in one hand, it may be said, a weapon in the other. At the quietest intervals, they had to be repairing their defences, shifting guns, carrying stores, burying the bodies of putrid animals. Constant false alarms kept them harassed before they had completed their works. For hours together the enemy sometimes went on shouting and sounding the advance, without showing themselves, so that all night the defenders, exhausted by the day's toil, might still have to stand on guard. Yet, overwrought as they were, small parties would here and there dash from their lines to spike a gun or drive away the occupants of some annoying outpost.

On our side there were many instances of daring prowess, but few of cowardice and shirking, as is testified by Lady Inglis. "As an example of brilliant courage, which to my mind made him one of the heroes of the siege, I must instance Private Cuney, H.M. 32nd. His exploits were marvellous; he was backed by a Sepoy named Kandial, who simply adored him. Single-handed and without any orders, Cuney would go outside our position, and he knew more of the enemy's movements than any one else. It was impossible to be really angry with him. Over and over again he was put into the guard-room for disobedience of orders, and as often let out when there was fighting to be done. On one occasion he surprised one of the enemy's batteries, into which he crawled, followed by his faithful Sepoy, bayoneting four men, and spiking the guns. If ever there was a man deserving the V.C., it was Cuney. He seemed to bear a charmed life. He was often wounded, and several times left his bed to volunteer for a sortie. He loved fighting for its own sake. After surviving the perils of the siege, he was at last killed in a sortie made after General Havelock's arrival."

Three weeks passed thus before the besiegers, swarming soon in tens of thousands around them, took courage for a general assault. The signal was an ineffectual explosion of a mine against the Redan battery; then from all sides they came pouring up to the works under cover of their cannon. But here every man was at his post to receive them desperately, many believing that their last hour was come. Some of the wounded had staggered out of hospital, pale and blood-stained, to lend a weak hand in the defence. The whole enclosure became quickly buried in sulphureous smoke, so that men hardly saw how the fight went in front of them, and still less knew but that their comrades had been overwhelmed at some other point, as well they might be, and whether at any moment the raging foe might not break in upon their rear. Again and again the Sepoys were urged on, to be mowed down by grape and musketry. Here they got right under our guns, driven away by hand grenades, bricks toppled over upon them, and whatever missiles came to hand; there they brought ladders against the walls, but were not allowed to make use of them. At one point, led on by the green standard of Islam in the hands of a reckless fanatic, they succeeded in bursting open a gate, only to block up the opening by their corpses. Four hours the din went on, under the fatal blaze of a July sun; but at length the enemy fled, leaving some thousands fallen round the unbroken walls, within which a surprisingly small number had been hurt.

This repulse put new heart into the victors, so much in need of cheering; and their spirits were soon raised still further by news of Havelock's army on its way to relieve them. They were not without communications from the outside world. An old pensioner named Unged several times managed to slip through the enemy's lines, bringing back messages and letters which were not always good news. Thus they had learned the fate of their kinsmen at Cawnpore; and their own temporary elation soon passed away under continued sufferings and losses.

The day after the assault, Major Banks was shot dead. Others who could be ill-spared fell one by one, every man placed *hors de combat* leaving more work to be done by his overstrained comrades. Then there were dissensions among the remaining leaders. The English soldiers, made reckless by peril, sometimes gave way to a spirit of insubordination, or disgraced themselves by drunkenness. The Sepoys could not be fully trusted. The enemy, there was reason to fear, had spies within the place to report its weak points and the embarrassment of its defenders. A proof of this was that they had ceased firing on the hospital when some native dignitaries, held as prisoners, were quartered there in the lucky thought of making them a shield for the sick. It was hard on those hostages, who had to take their share of the general want and peril. The rations of coarse beef and unground grain were found insufficient to keep the garrison in good case; and before long these had to be reduced, while the price of the smallest luxury had risen beyond the means of most. If a hen laid an egg it came as a god-send; a poor mother might have to beg in vain for a little milk for her dying child. What the English soldiers missed most was tobacco; and when some of the Sikhs deserted, they left a message that it was because they had no opium. The priceless Crown Jewels of Oudh, and the public treasure guarded in the Residency, were dross indeed in the eyes of men longing for the simplest comforts. How yearningly they fixed their eyes on the green gardens and parks blooming among the towers of Lucknow! And Havelock did not come to fulfil their hopes, soon dashed by news that he had been forced to fall back on Cawnpore, to recruit his own wasted forces.

At the beginning of August, our people had heard heavy firing and the sound of English music in the city, which brought them out cheering and shaking hands with each other on the tops of the houses, eager to catch the first sight of their approaching friends. That night they slept little, and rose to be bitterly disappointed. The rebels tauntingly derided this short-lived joy, shouting over the cause of yesterday's commotion. They had been saluting the boy crowned as puppet-king of Oudh. Their bands, indeed, were often heard playing familiar tunes, taught them in quieter days, and always wound up their concerts with "God Save the Queen!" which must have sounded a strange mockery in those English ears. Once it was the turn of the English to make a joyful demonstration, firing off a general salute on a report of the fall of Delhi, which turned out false, or at least premature.

On August 10, the Sepoys delivered another assault, but were more easily beaten off this time. It began by the explosion of a mine, which threw down the front of the Martinière post, ruining also some fifty feet of palisading and other bulwarks on each side. The assailants wanted boldness to master the breach thus made; but they lodged themselves in an underground room of this house, from which they had to be expelled by hand-grenades, dropped among them through a hole in the floor, and they got no further within the quickly-restored defences. At first, it is said, they could have walked in through an open door, which Mr. Schilling and his boys had the credit of shutting in their faces. The School would all have been blown up, but for the good fortune of having just been called in to prayers in an inner room. Three soldiers had been hurled by the explosion on to the enemy's ground, but ran back into the entrenchment, unhurt, under a shower of bullets.

The Sepoys' fire was kept up as hotly as ever, though at times they seemed to be badly off for shot, sending in such strange projectiles as logs of wood bound with iron, stones hollowed out for shells, twisted telegraph wires, copper coins and bullocks' horns; even the occasional use of bows and arrows lent a mediæval feature to the siege.

Their main effort now seemed directed to the destruction of the walls by mining. Here they were foiled, chiefly through the vigilance of Captain Fulton, an engineer-officer, who took a leading part in the defence, only to die before its end, like so many others. In the ranks of the 32nd, he found a number of old Cornish miners, with whose help he diligently countermined the subterranean attacks. Now the burrowing Sepoy broke through into an unsuspected aperture, to find Fulton patiently awaiting him, pistol in hand. Again, a deep-sunk gallery from within would be pushed so far, that our men blew up not only the enemy's mine, but a house full of his soldiers. The garrison had always their ears strained to catch those muffled blows, which announced new perils approaching them underground; then, as soon as the situation and direction of the mine could be recognized, Fulton went to work and the dusky pioneers either gave up the attempt or came on to their doom.

Once, however, they did catch the watchers at fault. At the corner of the defences called the Sikh Square, the warning sounds were mistaken for the trampling of horses tied up close by—a mistake first revealed by an explosion which made a breach in the works, overwhelming some of its defenders and hurling others into the air, most of whom came off with slight hurt. The Sepoys rushed on, but did not venture beyond the gap they had made, while some time passed before our men could dislodge them. One native officer was shot within the defences, the first and last time they were ever penetrated till they came to be abandoned. Of nearly forty mines attempted, this was the only one that could be called a success.

Several unhappy drummers, buried among the ruins, cried lamentably for assistance; but the risk of going to their assistance under fire was too great. A brave fellow did steal forward, and with a saw attempted to release one of the men held down by a beam across his chest, but the Sepoys drove him back when they saw what he was at. These half-buried lads had all died a miserable death of suffocation or thirst, if not from their injuries, when towards nightfall a party of the 32nd, shielding themselves behind bullet-proof shutters, advanced to recapture the lost ground at the point of the bayonet, which they not only did, and barricaded the breach with doors, but, while they were about it, made a dash forth to blow up some small houses that had given cover to the enemy.

This was one of several gallant sorties, in another of which Johannes' House was blown up, and the redoubtable "Bob the Nailer" killed in the act of exercising his deadly skill from the top of it. But his place as a marksman was taken by a brother negro of scarcely less fatal fame; and the enemy always expressed their resentment for these attacks by fresh bouts of more furious bombardment. Once, they had nearly destroyed a vital point of our line by piling up a bonfire against the Bailey Guard Gate; but Lieutenant R.H.M. Aitken, the burly Scot who held this post with his Sepoys, rushed out and extinguished the flames, under a rain of bullets, before much mischief could be done.

By this time the inmates of the Residency, from looking death so hard in the face, had grown strangely callous both to suffering and to danger. Men now showed themselves indifferent before the most heart-rending spectacles, while they coolly undertook perilous tasks at which, two months ago, the boldest would have hesitated. Children could be seen playing with grape-shot for marbles, and making little mines instead of mud-pies. Women took slight notice of the hair-breadth escapes that happened daily with them as with others. "Balls fall at our feet," says Mr. Rees in his journal, "and we continue the conversation without a remark; bullets graze our very hair, and we never speak of them. Narrow escapes are so very common that even women and children cease to notice them. They are the rule, not the exception. At one time a bullet passed through my hat; at another, I escaped being shot dead by one of the enemy's best riflemen, by an unfortunate soldier passing unexpectedly before me, and receiving the wound through the temples instead; at another, I moved off from a place where, in less than the twinkling of an eye afterwards, a musket-ball stuck in the wall. At another, again, I was covered with dust and pieces of brick by a round-shot that struck the wall not two inches away from me; at another, again, a shell burst a couple of yards away from me, killing an old woman and wounding a native boy and a native cook, one dangerously, the other slightly—but no; I must stop, for I could never exhaust the catalogue of hair-breadth escapes which every man in the garrison can speak of as well as myself."

Still, their hearts could not but grow heavy at times, especially as the feast of the Mohurrem drew near, when Moslem zeal might be expected to stimulate its votaries to more desperate fury. Desertions went on fast among the servants, and it was feared that, if relief came not soon, the Sepoys would go over to their mutinous comrades, who daily tried to seduce them with threats and promises. Some native Christians and half-castes, of whom better might have been expected, did run away in a body, only to be butchered by the fanatics among whom they so faithlessly cast their fortunes. A third of the Europeans had perished; the rest were worn with sickness and suffering, but they had not lost an inch of ground.

It was no fault of Havelock if he still lay at Cawnpore, forty miles away. Once and again he had advanced, beating the enemy every time they ventured to face him; but after two pitched battles, in which this fearless General had already had six horses killed under him, and several minor combats, the country-people rising up about him in fierce opposition, cholera also decimating the ranks, his losses were so heavy that he could not yet hope to force a way to Lucknow, much less through the narrow streets, where every house might be found a fortress.

Now reinforcements were being pushed up from Calcutta; and at the end of August, the besieged had a letter promising relief in twenty-five days. "Do not negotiate," was Havelock's warning to them, "but rather perish, sword in hand." So they meant to do, if it came to that, rather than fall alive into the power of such a cruel and treacherous foe. Meanwhile, there was nothing for it but to hold out doggedly till their deliverer could gather strength to reach them.

On September 5 the enemy tried another assault, which was more of a failure than ever. Evidently, on their side, they were losing heart. And at last, on the night of the 22nd, Unged, the trusty messenger, rushed into the entrenchment under fire, with news that Havelock and Outram were at hand. The latter's noble generosity here is one of his best titles to fame. He came to supersede the General who had so long strained every nerve in vain; but, knowing how Havelock had at heart the well-deserved honour of relieving Lucknow, the "Bayard of India," for the time, waived his own right to command, serving as a volunteer till this task should have been accomplished. In this, Sir James Outram afterwards judged himself to have done wrong, as putting sentiment before duty.

Two days of suspense followed, every ear within the Residency bent to catch the sound of the cannon of the advancing army. On the third day, the welcome din drew nearer, clouds of smoke marked the progress of a hot battle through the streets, and, as a hopeful sign, routed natives could be seen flying by hundreds, their bridges of boats breaking down under a confused mob of horsemen and foot-passengers, camels, elephants, and carriages. Havelock had forced the Char Bagh bridge of the canal, and was working round by its inner bank, to turn along the north side of the city, the ground here being more open. But all that long day lasted the doubt and the fear, as well as the joy, for our troops, their entrance once won into Lucknow, had to make a devious circuit about the most thickly-built quarters, and after all blunderingly fought their way, inch by inch, through the streets into a narrow winding road that led to the Residency. It was not till nightfall those strained eyes within could, by flashes of deadly fire, see the van of their countrymen struggling up to the riddled buildings, where—

"Ever upon the topmost roof our banner of England blew."

The struggling progress of the column is described, in a letter home, by Mr. Willock, a young civilian, who had volunteered to share its perils.

"The fire from the King's Palace, known as the 'Kaiser Bagh,' was so severe that we had to run double-quick in front of it, as hard as we could; and a scene of great confusion ensued when we halted—guns and infantry mixed up, soldiers wandering in search of their companies, and the wounded in the dhoolies carried here and there without any orders. We had been there about half-an-hour when the Second Brigade joined us, passing in front of the palace, emerging from a narrow lane close to it. Here they had to pass under the very walls, while the rebels on the walls hurled down stones and bricks, and even spat at our fellows, a fierce fire being kept up from the loop-holes. After a little time order was re-established, and after a fresh examination of the map, the column was drawn up, and we started again. It was cruel work—brave troops being exposed to such unfair fighting. What can men do against loop-holed houses, when they have no time to enter a city, taking house by house? In fact, we ran the gauntlet regularly through the streets.

"After we passed the Palace, our men were knocked down like sheep, without being able to return the fire of the enemy with any effect. We passed on some little way, when we came to a sudden turning to the left, with a huge gateway in front, and through this we had to pass, under a shower of balls from the houses on each side. The Sikhs and 5th Fusiliers got to the front, and kept up a steady fire at the houses for some time, with the hope of lessening the enemy's musketry fire, but it was no use. Excited men can seldom fire into loop-holes with any certainty, and we had to make the best of our way up the street, turning sharp round to the right, when we found ourselves in a long, wide street, with sheets of fire shooting out from the houses. On we went, about a quarter of a mile, being peppered from all sides, when suddenly we found ourselves opposite to a large gateway, with folding doors completely riddled with round-shot and musket-balls, the entrance to a large enclosure.

"At the side of this was a small doorway, half blocked up by a low mud wall; the Europeans and Sikhs were struggling to get through, while the bullets were whistling about them. I could not think what was up, and why we should be going in there; but after forcing my way up to the door, and getting my head and shoulders over the wall, I found myself being pulled over by a great unwashed hairy creature,[6] who set me on my legs and patted me on the back, and, to my astonishment, I found myself in the 'Bailey Guard!'"

The scene then ensuing has been often described—the garrison pressing forward with cheers of welcome and triumph—the rough Highlanders suddenly appearing through the darkness among the ruins they had fought so many battles to save—their begrimed faces running with tears in the torchlight, as they caught up in their arms the pale children, and kissed their country-women, too, in that spasm of glad emotion; even the ladies ready to hug them for hysteric joy—the gaunt, crippled figures tottering out to join in the general rejoicing, now that for a moment all believed their trials at an end. That picturesque incident of a Highland Jessie, first to catch the distant strains of the bagpipes, appears to be a fiction. But bagpipes were not wanting; and one of the defenders, strolling over as soon as he could leave his own post, hardly able to believe the good news true, tells us how he found dancing going on to the music of two Highland pipers—a demonstration, however, soon put a stop to by Havelock's orders.

Havelock had cause to think this no time for dancing. While the common soldiers might exult over their melodramatic victory, the leaders knew too well at what a cost it had been won, and what dangers still encompassed them. Not all the little army of two thousand five hundred men had pushed through on that memorable evening. Nearly a fifth part of them were lost in the attempt. Neill had been shot dead, with the goal already in sight. Outram himself was hurt. It had been necessary to leave most of the wounded on the way, many of whom, deserted by the natives who bore their litters, suffered a horrible fate, massacred or burned alive while their comrades were making merry within the works. Part of the relieving force bivouacked all night on the road outside, where in the confusion a lamentable affair occurred, some of our faithful Sepoys at the Bailey Gate being attacked in mistake by the excited new-comers.

Only two days later, the rear-guard, hampered by the heavy guns, could join its commander at the Residency; and even then a force, in charge of baggage and

[6] This "great unwashed hairy creature" appears to have been "Jock" Aitken, in whom, as his kinsman, the author must own to a special interest. A monument to him now stands by the post he guarded so well.

ammunition, was left besieged in the Alum Bagh, a fortified park beyond the city, which henceforth became an isolated English outpost.

The relieving army had been hurried on at all risks, under a mistaken belief that the garrison was in immediate straits of famine. It turned out they had still food to last some weeks, even with so many more mouths to fill, an unreckoned store of grain having been found heaped up, by Lawrence's foresight, in the plunge-bath below the Residency. Means of transport, however, were wanting; and Outram, who now assumed command, could not undertake to fight his way out again with the encumbrance of a long train of non-combatants. Much less was he in a position to clear the city, still occupied by the enemy in overwhelming numbers. All he could do was to hold on where he was, awaiting the arrival of another army now on the march.

It was a relief and not a rescue over which so much jubilation had been spent. It came just in time, now that the fall of Delhi had set free a swarm of Sepoys to swell the ranks of the Lucknow besiegers. The mere sight of their countrymen, and the sure news they brought, was enough to put fresh spirit into the defenders, who, by the help of such a reinforcement, no longer doubted to hold the fortress that had sheltered them for three miserable months, with the loss of more than seven hundred combatants by death and desertion.

Here, then, the siege entered upon a second period, the characteristic of which was an extended position occupied by the garrison. Now that they had plenty of men, they seized some of the adjacent palaces, and pushed their lines down to the river-bank. Like men risen from a long sickness, they stretched their legs on the ground that for weeks had been raining death into their enclosure. There must have been a strange satisfaction in strolling out from their own half-ruined abodes, to examine the damage they had wrought among the enemy's works, at the risk of an occasional shot from his new posts, as the Martinière boys found when they let curiosity get the better of caution.

Some of these youngsters soon managed to run into mischief. A few days after the relief, being sent out to pick up firewood among the *débris*, they stole a look where still lay the mutilated corpses of Havelock's wounded men murdered so basely, then rambled into one of the royal palaces—a labyrinth of courts, gardens, gateways, passages, pavilions, verandahs, halls, and so forth, all in the bewildering style of Eastern magnificence, where it was difficult not to lose one's way. Here a general plunder was going on, and our people, even gleaning after the Sepoys, could help themselves freely to silks, satins, velvets, cloth of gold, embroideries, costly brocade, swords, books, pictures, and all sorts of valuables. In some rooms were nothing but boxes full of gorgeous china, ransacked so eagerly that the floors soon became covered a foot deep with broken crockery. Others of the besieged pounced most willingly upon articles of food, especially on tea, tobacco, and vegetables, which to them seemed treasures indeed. For their part, the Martinière boys ferreted out a store of fireworks, and must needs set off some rockets towards the enemy. One of these dangerous playthings, however, exploded in their hands, kindling others and setting fire to the building. The boys scampered out without being noticed, and took care to hold their tongues about this adventure, so that it was not ascertained at the time, though strongly suspected, on whom to lay the blame of a conflagration that went on for several days. The former King of Oudh who built this costly pile, little thought how one day its glories were to perish by the idle hands of a pack of careless school-boys.

The trials of the garrison were by no means over. Sickness continued to make havoc among them for want of wholesome food, especially of vegetables, the best part of their diet being tough artillery bullocks. The smallest luxury was still at famine price. The cold weather drawing on found many of these poor people ill-provided with clothing. One officer had gained asylum here in such a ragged state, that he was fain to make himself a suit of clothes from the green cloth of the Residency billiard-table. All were heartily sick of confinement and anxiety. Yet nearly two months more had to be passed in a state of blockade, the enemy no longer at such close quarters, but still bombarding them with his artillery, and keeping them on the alert by persistent attempts to mine their defences.

They were now, however, able to do more than stand on the defensive, making vigorous sallies, before which the Sepoys readily gave way, and held their own ground only by the weight of numbers. Good news, too, cheered the inmates of this ark of refuge. All round them the flood of mutiny seemed to be subsiding. Delhi had fallen at length, while they still held their shattered asylum. Sir Colin Campbell was coming to make a clean sweep of the rebel bands who kept Oudh in fear and confusion. The heroes of Lucknow knew for certain that they were not forgotten by their countrymen. They could trust England to be proud of them, and felt how every heart at home would now be throbbing with the emotion, which the Laureate was one day to put into deathless verse.

> "Men will forget what we suffer and not what we do. We can fight—
> But to be soldier all day and be sentinel all through the night!
> Ever the mine and assault, our sallies, their lying alarms,
> Bugles and drums in the darkness, and shoutings and soundings to arms;
> Ever the labour of fifty that had to be done by five;
> Ever the marvel among us that one should be left alive;
> Ever the day with its traitorous death from the loop-holes around;
> Ever the night with its coffinless corpse to be laid in the ground.
>
> * * * * *
>
> Grief for our perishing children, and never a moment for grief;
> Toil and ineffable weariness, faltering hopes of relief;
> Havelock baffled, or beaten, or butchered for all that we knew.
> Then day and night, night and day, coming down on the still shattered walls,
> Millions of musket bullets and thousands of cannon balls—
> But ever upon the topmost roof our banner of England blew."

# CHAPTER VIII

## LORD CLYDE'S CAMPAIGNS

Sir Colin Campbell, soon to earn the title of Lord Clyde, had arrived at Calcutta in the middle of August, as Commander-in-Chief of an army still on its way from England by the slow route of the Cape. He could do nothing for the moment but stir up the authorities in providing stores and transport for his men when they came to hand. All the troops available in Bengal were needed to guard the disarmed Sepoys here, and to keep clear the six hundred miles of road to Allahabad, infested as it was by flying bands of mutineers and robbers. But if he had no English soldiers to command, there was a brigade of sailors, five hundred strong, who under their daring leader, Captain William Peel, steamed up the Ganges, ahead of the army, to which more than once they were to show the way on an unfamiliar element.

In the course of next month, arrived the troops of the intercepted China expedition, a detachment from the Cape, and other bodies coming in by driblets, who were at once forwarded to Allahabad, part of the way by rail and then by bullock-trains. A considerable force of Madras Sepoys, more faithful than their Bengal comrades, was also at the disposal of the Government, and helped to restore order in the country about the line of march, still so much agitated that reinforcements moving to the front were apt to be turned aside to put down local disturbances. Sir Colin himself, hurrying forward along the Grand Trunk Road, had almost been captured by a party of rebels.

On November 1, he was at Allahabad, from which his troops were already pushing on towards Cawnpore, not without an encounter, where the Naval Brigade won their first laurels on land. Two days later, Sir Colin reached Cawnpore, and at once had to make a choice of urgent tasks. To his left, the state of Central India had become threatening. The revolted Gwalior Contingent Sepoys, in the service of Scindia, had long been kept inactive by their nominal master; but after the fall of Delhi, they marched against us under Tantia Topee, the Mahratta chief who had carried out the massacre at Cawnpore, and now comes forward as one of the chief generals on the native side. This army, swollen by bands from Delhi, approached to menace the English communications on the Ganges, if it were not faced before our men turned to the right for the relief of Lucknow. The question was, whether or not to deal with Tantia Topee at once. But Sir Colin, misled like Havelock by a false estimate of the provisions in the Residency, decided at all risks to lose no time in carrying off the garrison there, even though he must leave a powerful enemy in his rear. Over and over again in this war, English generals had to neglect the most established rules of strategy, trusting to the ignorance or the cowardice of their opponents. Yet Tantia Topee showed himself a leader who could by no means be trusted for failing to improve his opportunities.

Leaving behind him, then, five hundred Europeans and a body of Madras Sepoys, under General Windham, to hold the passage of the Ganges at Cawnpore, the Commander-in-Chief marched northwards to join Sir Hope Grant, awaiting him with a column released from Delhi; and the combined force moved upon the Alum Bagh, still held by a detachment of Outram's force. From this point they were able to communicate with the Residency by means of a semaphore telegraph erected on its roof, worked according to the instructions of the *Penny Cyclopædia*, which happened to be in the hands of the besieged. Native messengers also passed to and fro, through whom Outram had generously recommended the relieving army to attack Tantia Topee first, letting his garrison hold out upon reduced rations, as he thought they could do till the end of November. He had thus furnished Sir Colin with plans of the city and directions that would be most useful to the latter as a stranger. But it seemed important to give him some guide fully to be trusted for more precise information as to the localities through which he must make his attack. A bold civilian, named Kavanagh, volunteered to go from the Residency to the camp, on this dangerous errand, by which he well-earned the Victoria Cross.

In company with a native, himself dyed and disguised as one of the desperadoes who swarmed about Lucknow, Kavanagh left our lines by swimming over the river, re-crossed it by a bridge, and walked through the chief street, meeting few people, none of whom recognized him for a European. Outside the city, the two companions lost their way, but were actually set right by a picket of the rebels, who here and there challenged them or let them pass without notice. Before daybreak they fell in with the British outposts, and at noon a flag on the Alum Bagh informed the garrison of their emissary's safe arrival.

On November 12, Sir Colin reached the Alum Bagh, where he spent one more day in making final arrangements; then, on the 14th, he set out to begin the series of combats by which he must reach a hand to our beleaguered countrymen. His army, with reinforcements coming up at the last moment from Cawnpore, numbered some five thousand men and fifty guns, made up in great part of fragments of several regiments, the backbone of it the 93rd Highlanders, fresh from England, and steeled by the Crimean battles in which they had learned to trust their present leader. These precious lives had to be husbanded for further pressing work; and in any case he naturally sought a safer road than that on which Havelock had lost a third of his force.

One looking at the map of Lucknow might be puzzled to explain the circuitous route taken by both generals from the Alum Bagh to the Residency, which stand directly opposite each other on either side of the city, some three or four miles apart. Running a gauntlet of street-fighting was the main peril to be avoided. Then, not only should the approach be made as far as possible through open suburbs, but while the Residency quarter is bounded by the windings of the Goomtee to the north, the south and east sides are defended by the Canal, a deep curved ravine, in the wet season filled with water. Instead of forcing his way, like Havelock, over its nearest bridge, Sir Colin meant to make a sweep half-round the city on the further side of this channel, taking the rebels by surprise at an unexpected point, as well as hoping to avoid the fire of the Kaiser Bagh, a huge royal palace, which was their head-quarters, and commanded the usual road to the Residency.

His first move was to the Dilkoosha, a hunting palace with a walled enclosure, which he fortified as a depôt for his stores and for the great train of vehicles provided to carry off the women and children. The same day he seized the Martinière College close by, and pushed his position towards the banks of the Canal, from their side of which the enemy made hostile demonstrations. Next day was spent in final arrangements and in repelling attacks. By ostentatious activity in that direction, the Sepoys were led to believe that they would be assailed on the English left; but on the morning of the 16th Sir Colin marched off by his right, crossed the bed of the Canal, dry at this point, gained the bank of the river, and penetrated the straggling suburbs upon the enemy's rear, with no more than three thousand men, the rest left posted so as to keep open his retreat. A small force this for a week's fighting, under most difficult circumstances,against enormous odds, where a way must again and again be opened through fortified buildings!

**The Kaiserbagh, Lucknow.**

**Ruins of the Residency, Lucknow.**

The line of march lay along narrow winding lanes and through woods and mud walls, that for a time sheltered our troops from fire. The first obstacle encountered was the Secunder Bagh, one of those walled gardens which played such a part in the operations about Lucknow and Delhi. Its gloomy ruins stand to-day to tell a dreadful tale. The approaches had first to be cleared, and the walls battered by guns that could hardly be forced up a steep bank under terrible fire. In half-an-hour, a small hole had been knocked through one gate, then, Highlanders and Sikhs racing to be foremost in the fierce assault, the enclosure was carried, where two thousand mutineers were caught as in a trap. Some fought desperately to the last; some threw down their arms begging for mercy, but found no mercy in hearts maddened by the remembrance of slaughtered women and children. "Cawnpore!" was the cry with which our men drove their bayonets home; and when the wild din of fire and sword, of shrieks and curses, at length fell silent, this pleasure-garden ran with the blood of two thousand dusky corpses, piled in heaps or strewn over every foot of ground. We may blame the spirit of barbaric revenge; but we had not seen that well at Cawnpore.

The advance was now resumed across a plain dotted by houses and gardens, where soon it came once more to a stand before the Shah Nujeef, a mosque surrounded with high loop-holed walls, that proved a harder nut to crack than the

Secunder Bagh. For hours it was battered and assaulted in vain, the General himself leading his Highlanders to the charge. In vain the guns of Peel's Naval Brigade were once brought up within a few yards of the walls, worked as resolutely as if their commander had been laying his ship beside an enemy's. In vain brave men rushed to their death at those fiery loop-holes, while behind them reigned a scene of perilous confusion, the soldiers able neither to advance nor retreat among blazing buildings and deadly missiles. The narrow road had become choked up by the train of camels and other animals, so that ammunition could scarcely be forced to the front. From the opposite side of the river, the enemy brought a heavy gun to bear upon the disordered ranks. Our batteries had to be withdrawn under cover of a searching rocket-fire.

For a moment Sir Colin feared all might be lost. Yet, after all, what seems little better than an accident put an easy end to this desperate contest. At nightfall, a sergeant of the 93rd, prowling round the obstinate wall, discovered a fissure through which the Highlanders tore their way, to see the white-clad Sepoys flitting out through the smoke before them. Our men could now lie down on their arms, happy to think that the worst part of the task was over.

Next morning, the same laborious and deadly work went on. Other large buildings had to be hastily bombarded and a way broken through them, in presence of a host strong enough to surround the scanty force. But this day the amazed enemy seemed to have his hands too full to interfere much with our progress. Parties had been thrown out towards the city, on Sir Colin's left, to form a chain of posts which should cover his advance and secure his retreat. Meanwhile, also, the garrison of the Residency were busy on their side, with mines and sorties, pushing forward to meet the relieving army, who spent most of the day in breaching a building known as the Mess House. This was at length carried, as well as a palace beyond, called the Motee Mahal, by gallant assaults, foremost in which were two of our most illustrious living soldiers, Lord Wolseley and Sir Frederick Roberts.

Between the relievers and the defences of the Residency there now remained only a few hundred yards of open space, swept by the guns of the Kaiser Bagh. Mr. Kavanagh appears to have been the first man who reached the garrison with his good news; then Outram and Havelock rode forward under hot fire to meet Sir Colin Campbell on that hard won battle-field, over which for days they had been anxiously tracing his slow progress.

This relief may seem to fall short of the dramatic effect of Havelock's, though it has grand features of its own, and from a military point of view is a more admirable achievement. To many of the beleaguered it brought a sore disappointment, when they learned that their countrymen had come only to carry them away, and that, after all, they must abandon this already famous citadel to the foe they had so long kept at bay by their own strength—the one spot in Oudh where the English flag had never been lowered throughout all the perils of the rebellion. Inglis offered to go on holding the place against any odds, if left with six hundred men and due supplies; but Sir Colin, while admiring his spirit, was in no mind for sentiment, aware that not a man could be spared to idle defiance. At first he had been for giving them only two hours to prepare their departure. A delay of a few days, however, was won from or forced upon him by the circumstances to be reckoned with—days to him full of anxious responsibility, and for his men of fresh perils.

On Nov. 19, a hot fire was opened against the Kaiser Bagh, the enemy thus led to believe in an assault imminent here. Under cover of this demonstration, the non-combatants were first moved out in small groups behind the screen of posts held through the suburbs, all reaching the Dilkoosha safely. At midnight of the 22nd the soldiers followed, the covering posts withdrawn as they passed, and the whole force was brought off without the loss of a man, while the Sepoys blinded their own eyes by continuing to bombard the deserted entrenchment. The garrison were naturally loth to leave it a prey to such a foe, who could neither drive them out nor prevent them from marching away before his face. They had to abandon most of their belongings to be plundered, the army being already too much hampered by its train. The public treasure, however, was carried off, and the Sepoys so far disappointed of a prize they had striven in vain to wrest from these poor works. The guns also had been saved or rendered unserviceable. It was trying work for the women, their road being at some points under fire, so that they had to catch up the children and make a run for it; then, once behind safe walls again, they must wait two or three days in suspense for husbands and fathers, who might have to cut their way out, if the Sepoys became aware what was going on.

Among the first to leave were the Martinière boys, whom we have left out of sight for a time. Some of these juvenile heroes, however, had been too eager about getting away. The elder ones, who carried arms, forgot that they were numbered as soldiers, and must wait for orders before retiring. Next day they had a sharp hint of this in being arrested and sent back under escort to the Residency, where a bold face of defence was still maintained, the enemy to be kept in ignorance of our proposed retreat. We may suppose that the young deserters were let off easily; and, on the day after, Hilton and another boy, having satisfied military punctilio, obtained an honourable exit by being sent off in charge of two ponies conveying money and other valuable property belonging to the College. On the way they came under fire of an enemy's battery across the river, and a shot whizzed so near that the ponies ran off and upset their precious burden; then the boys, helped by some of Peel's sailors, who were replying to the Sepoy fire, had much ado in picking up the rupees and catching their restive beasts; but, without further adventure, once more reached the camp at Dilkoosha, where, with plenty to eat, and the new sense of being able to eat it in safety, they could listen to the roar of guns still resounding in the city.

The final scene is described for us by Captain Birch, who had throughout acted as aide-de-camp to Inglis:—"First, the garrison in immediate contact with the enemy, at the furthest extremity of the Residency position, was marched out. Every other garrison in turn fell in behind it, and so passed out through the Bailey Guard Gate, till the whole of our position was evacuated. Then came the turn of Havelock's force, which was similarly withdrawn post by post, marching in rear of our garrison. After them again came the forces of the Commander-in-Chief, which joined on in the rear of Havelock's force. Regiment by regiment was withdrawn with the utmost order and regularity. The whole operation resembled the movement of a telescope. Stern silence was kept, and the enemy took no alarm. Never shall I forget that eventful night. The withdrawal of the fourteen garrisons which occupied our defensive positions was entrusted to three staff-officers—Captain Wilson, assistant Adjutant-General; the Brigade-Major, and myself, as aide-de-camp. Brigadier Inglis stood at the Bailey Guard Gate as his gallant garrison defiled past him; with him was Sir James Outram, commanding the division. The night was dark, but on our side, near the Residency-house, the hot gun-metal from some guns, which we burst before leaving, set fire to the heap of wood used as a rampart, which I have before described, and lighted up the place. The noise of the bursting of the guns, and the blazing of the rampart, should have set the enemy on the *qui vive*, but they took no notice. Somehow, a doubt arose whether the full tale of garrisons had passed the gate. Some counted thirteen, and some fourteen; probably two had got mixed; but, to make certain, I was sent back to Innes' post, the furthest garrison, to see if all had been withdrawn. The utter stillness and solitude of the deserted position, with which I was so familiar, struck coldly on my nerves; I had to go, and go I did. Had the enemy known of our departure, they would ere this have occupied our places, and there was also a chance of individuals or single parties having got in for the sake of plunder; but I did not meet a living soul. I think I may fairly claim to have seen the last of the Residency of Lucknow before its abandonment to the enemy. Captain Waterman, 13th Native Infantry, however, was the last involuntarily to leave; he fell asleep after his name had been called, and woke up to find himself alone; he escaped in safety, but the fright sent him off his head for a time. As I made my report to the commanders at the gate, Sir James Outram waved his hand to Brigadier Inglis to precede him in departure, but the Brigadier stood firm, and claimed to be the last to leave the ground which he and his gallant regiment had so stoutly defended. Sir James Outram smiled, then, extending his hand, said, 'Let us go out together;' so, shaking hands, these two heroic spirits, side by side, descended the declivity outside our battered gate. Immediately behind them came the staff, and the place of honour again became the subject of dispute between Captain Wilson and myself; but the former was weak from all the hardships and privations he had undergone, and could not stand the trick of shoulder to shoulder learned in the Harrow football fields. Prone on the earth he lay, till he rolled down the hill, and I was the last of the staff to leave the Bailey Guard Gate."

On the 23rd all were united at the Dilkoosha; but here the successful retreat became overclouded by a heavy loss. Havelock, worn out through care and disease, died before he could know of the honours bestowed upon him by his grateful countrymen, yet happy in being able to say truly: "I have for forty years so ruled my life that, when death came, I might face it without fear." Under a tree, marked only with a rudely scrawled initial, he was left buried at the Alum Bagh, till a prouder monument should signalize his grave as one of the many holy spots "where England's patriot soldiers lie."

There was no time then for mourning. Leaving Outram with a strong detachment at the Alum Bagh, to keep Lucknow in check, Sir Colin hurried by forced marches to Cawnpore, where his bridge of boats across the Ganges was now in serious danger. As the long train of refugees approached it, they were again greeted by the familiar sound of cannon, telling how hard a little band of English troops fought to keep open for them the way to safety. The city was in flames, and a hot battle going on beyond the river, when Sir Colin appeared upon the scene, not an hour too soon, for his small force here had been driven out of its camp into the entrenchment covering the bridge. "Our soldiers do not withdraw well," an observer drily remarked of this almost disastrous affair.

Next day, he crossed the Ganges to confront Tantia Topee with less unequal force. Before doing anything more, he must get rid of his encumbering charge, some of whom had died in the haste of that anxious march. On December 3, the non-combatants were sent off towards Allahabad, on carriages or on foot, till they came to the unfinished railway, and had what was for many of them their first experience of railroad travelling. As soon as they were well out of danger, on December 6, was fought the third battle of Cawnpore, which ended in a disastrous rout of the rebels.

This victory could not be immediately followed up, owing to want of transport, the carriages having been sent off to Allahabad. But Sir Colin now felt himself master of the situation, with also the "cold weather," as it is called by comparison, in favour of English soldiers, and laid his plans for thoroughly reconquering the country, step by step. We need not track all his careful movements, which lasted through the winter, and indeed beyond the end of next year; it would be a too tedious repetition of hopeless combats and flights on the part of the enemy, hiding and running before our forces, who eagerly sought every chance of bringing them to bay. The dramatic interest of the story is largely gone, now that its end becomes a foregone conclusion. So leaving Sir Colin and his lieutenants to sweep the Doab, we return next spring to see him make an end of Lucknow, which all along figures so prominently in these troubles. It was here that the rebellion died hardest, since in Oudh it had more the character of a popular rising, and not of a mere military mutiny.

The Commander-in-Chief would have preferred to go on with a slow and sure conquest of Rohilcund, letting Lucknow blaze itself out for the meanwhile; but the Governor-General urged him to a speedy conquest of that city, for the sake of the prestige its mastership gave, so much value being attached to the superficial impressions of power we could make on the native mind. As it was, Sir Colin thought well to wait, through most of the cold weather, for the arrival of reinforcements, in part still delayed by the task of restoring order on the way. Then also he was expecting a slow Goorkha army under Jung Bahadoor, the ruler of Nepaul, who, having offered his assistance, might take offence if the siege were begun without him. The newspapers and other irresponsible critics attacked our general for what seemed strange inaction. Indeed, he was judged over-cautious by officers who with a few hundreds of English soldiers had seen exploits accomplished such as he delayed to undertake with thousands. He at least justified himself by final success, and none have a right to blame him who do not know the difficulty of assembling and providing for the movements of an army where every European soldier needs the services of natives and beasts of burden, and every animal, too, must have at least one attendant.

It was not till the beginning of March that he set out from Cawnpore with the strongest British force ever seen in India—twenty thousand soldiers, followed by a train fourteen miles long; camels, elephants, horses, ponies, goats, sheep, dogs, and even poultry, with stores and tents; litters for the sick in the rear of each regiment; innumerable servants, grooms, grass-cutters, water-carriers, porters, traders and women—a motley crowd from every part of India; and over all a hovering cloud of kites and vultures, ready to swoop down on the refuse of this moving multitude and the carnage that would soon mark its advance. As it dragged its slow length along, moreover, the army now unwound a trail of telegraph wire, through which its head could at any moment communicate with his base of operations, and with Lord Canning, who had made Allahabad the seat of his Government, to be nearer the field.

Yet such a force was small enough to assail a hostile city some score of miles in circuit, holding a population estimated at from half a million upwards, and a garrison that, with revolted troops and fierce swashbucklers, was believed to be still over a hundred thousand strong. Their leaders were a woman and a priest—the Moulvie, who at the outset became notorious by preaching a religious war against us infidels, then all along appears to have been the animating spirit of that protracted struggle; and the Begum, mother of a boy set up as King of Oudh. This poor lad got little good out of his kingship; and even those in real authority about him must have had their hands full in trying to control his turbulent subjects.

But there was some military rule among the rebels, and during the winter they had been diligent in fortifying their huge stronghold. A high earthen parapet, like a railway embankment, had been thrown up along the banks of the Canal, itself a valuable defence, now rendered impassable where Sir Colin crossed before, with trenches and rifle-pits beyond; inside this a line of palaces connected by earthworks formed a second barrier; and the citadel was the Kaiser Bagh, a vast square of courtyards crowned by battlements, spires and cupolas, gilt or glaringly painted—a semi-barbaric Versailles. This, though it had no great strength in itself, was put in a position of defence. The chief streets were blocked by barriers or stockades, and the houses loop-holed and otherwise turned to account as fortifications wherever the assailants might be expected to force their way. Still, after the exploits again and again performed by handfuls against hosts, there was no one in our army who now for a moment doubted of success.

As they approached that doomed city, the English soldiers were greeted by the cannon of the Alum Bagh, where all winter Outram, with four thousand men, had coolly held himself in face of such a swarm of enemies. On March 4th, Sir Colin was encamped in the parks about the Dilkoosha, from the roof of which he surveyed the wide prospect of palaces and gardens before him, while his outposts kept up a duel of artillery and musketry with the Martinière opposite, where the rebels had established themselves. He soon saw the weak point in their scheme of defence. They had omitted to fortify the city on its north side, supposing this to be protected sufficiently by the river, the two permanent bridges of which were a long way up, beyond the Residency, and approached on the further bank through straggling suburbs. Here, then, the enemy not being prepared, was the best place to attack; and though before more resolute and skilful opponents, it would be counted rash to separate the two wings of an army by a deep river, under the circumstances, this was what Sir Colin resolved to do. A pontoon-bridge was thrown across the Goomtee, by which, on the 6th, Outram crossed with a column of all arms, to encamp near Chinhut, the scene of our reverse under Sir Henry Lawrence.

The next two days were spent in pushing back the enemy, who had soon discovered Outram's movements; and by the morning of the 9th, he had established himself on the left side of the river, with a battery enfilading the rear of the first defensive line running from its right bank. Just as the guns were about to open fire, it appeared that the rebels had not stayed for any further hint to be off. On the opposite side could be seen a detachment of Highlanders waiting to carry the abandoned wall. Shouts and gestures failing to attract their attention, a brave young officer volunteered to swim over the river to make certain how matters stood; and presently a dripping figure was seen on the top of the parapet, beckoning up the Highlanders, who rushed in to find the works here abandoned to them without a blow. The Martinière, close by, was carried with almost equal ease, the Sepoys swarming out like rats from a sinking ship; and thus quickly a footing had already been gained in those elaborate defences. Before the day was over, we held the enemy's first line of defence.

For another two days, the operations went on without a check, Outram advancing on the opposite side as far as the bridges and bombarding the works in the city from flank and rear, while Sir Colin took and occupied, one by one, the strong buildings, some of which, already familiar to his companions in the former attack, were found still tainted by the corpses of its victims, but this time gave not so much trouble. Jung Bahadoor now arrived with his Goorkhas, enabling the line of assault to be extended to the left. Two more days, Sir Colin sapped and stormed his way through fortified buildings on the open ground between the river and the city, choosing this slow progress rather than expose his men to the risk of street-fighting. On the 14th, the third line of works was seized, and our men pressed eagerly forward into the courts and gardens of the Kaiser Bagh, which at once fell into their hands with some confused slaughter.

This rapid success came so unexpectedly, that no arrangements had been made for restraining the triumphant soldiery from such a wild orgy of spoil and destruction as now burst loose through that spacious pleasure-house. The scene has been vividly described by Dr. Russell, the *Times* Correspondent, who was an eye-witness—walls broken down, blazing or ball-pitted; statues and fountains reddened with blood; dead or dying Sepoys in the orange-groves and summer-houses; at every door a crowd of powder-grimed soldiers blowing open the locks, or smashing the panels with the butt ends of their muskets; their officers in vain trying to recall them to discipline; the men, "drunk with plunder," smashing vases and mirrors, ripping up pictures, making bonfires of costly furniture, tearing away gems from their setting, breaking open lids, staggering out loaded with porcelain, tapestry, caskets of jewels, splendid arms and robes, strangely disguised in shawls and head-dresses of magnificent plumes. Even parrots, monkeys, and other tame animals were made part of the booty. One man offered Dr. Russell for a hundred rupees a chain of precious stones afterwards sold for several thousand pounds; another was excitedly carrying off a string of glass prisms from a chandelier, taking them for priceless emeralds; some might be seen swathed in cloth of gold, or flinging away too cumbrous treasures that would have been a small fortune to them. This wasteful robbery broke loose while the din of shots and yells still echoed through the battered walls and labyrinthine corridors of the palace. Then, as fresh bands poured in to share the loot, white men and black, these comrades had almost turned their weapons on each other in the rage of greed; and, meantime, without gathered a crowd of more timid but not less eager camp-followers, waiting till the lions had gorged themselves, to fall like jackals upon the leavings of the spoil. To this had come the rich magnificence of the kings of Oudh.

Amid such distraction, the victors thought little of following up their routed enemy, whose ruin, however, would have been overwhelming had Outram, as was his own wish, now crossed the nearest bridge to fall upon the mass of dismayed fugitives. Sir Colin had given him leave to do so on condition of not losing a single man—an emphatic caution, perhaps not meant to be taken literally; but Outram, whom nobody could suspect of failing in hardihood, interpreted it as keeping him inactive. Thus a great number of rebels now made their escape, scattering over the country. Many still clung to the further buildings, which remained to be carried. Even two days later some of them had the boldness to sally out against our rear at the Alum Bagh, and the Moulvie, their leader, did not take flight for some days. But, after the capture of the chief palace, the rest could be only a matter of time.

By the end of a week, with little further opposition, on March 21, we had mastered the whole city, to find it almost deserted by its terrified inhabitants, after enjoying for almost a year the doubtful benefits of independence.

The British soldiers were now lodged in the palaces of Oudh, and might stroll admiringly through the ruins of that wretched fortress which, in the hands of their countrymen, had held out as many months as it had taken them days to overcome the formidable works of the enemy. Their victory was followed up by a proclamation from the Governor-General, that in the opinion of many seemed harsh and unwise, since, with a few exceptions, it declared the lands of Oudh forfeit to the conquering power. The natural tendency of this was to drive the dispossessed nobles and landowners into a guerilla warfare, in which they were supported by the rebels escaped from Lucknow to scatter over the country, taking as strongholds the forts and jungles that abound in it. Nearly a year, indeed, passed before Oudh was fully pacified.

After sending out columns to deal with some of the most conspicuous points of danger, Sir Colin moved into Rohilcund, his next task being the reduction of its no less contumacious population. On May 5th, a sharp fight decided the fate of Bareilly, its capital. Then he was recalled by the Oudh rebels, growing to some head again under that persistent foe the Moulvie. But, next month, the Moulvie fell in a petty affray with some of his own countrymen—a too inglorious end for one of our most hearty and determined opponents, who seems to have had the gifts of a leader as well as of a preacher of rebellion.

Again may be hurried over a monotonous record of almost constant success. The troops had suffered so frightfully from heat, that they must now be allowed a little repose through the rainy season. With next winter began the slow work of hunting down the rebels, in which Sir Hope Grant took a leading part. By the spring of 1859, those still in arms had been driven into Nepaul, or forced to take shelter in the pestilential, tiger-haunted jungles of the Terai, while throughout Hindostan burned bungalows were rebuilding, broken telegraph-posts replacing, officials coming back to their stations; and the machinery of law and order became gradually brought again into gear, under the dread of a race that could so well assert its supremacy.

# CHAPTER IX

## THE EXTINCTION

It has been impossible to note all the minor operations in this confused war, and the isolated risings of which here and there we have caught glimpses through the clouds of smoke overhanging the main field of action—a mere corner of India, yet a region as large as England. Thrills of sympathetic disaffection ran out towards Assam on the one side, and to Goojerat on the other; up northwards into the Punjaub, as we have seen, then through the Central Provinces, down into Bombay, and to the great native state of Hyderabad, where the Nizam and his shrewd minister Salar Jung managed to keep their people quiet, yet reverses on our part might at any time have inflamed them beyond restraint.

Among the protected or semi-independent Courts of Rajpootana and Central India there were serious troubles. Scindia and Holkar, the chief Mahratta princes, stood loyal to us; but their soldiery took the other side. The most remarkable case of hostility here was that of the Ranee or Queen of Jhansi, a dispossessed widow, who had much the same grievance against the British Government as Nana Sahib, and avenged it by similar treacherous cruelty. She managed to blind the small English community to their danger till the Sepoys broke out early in June with the usual excesses; then our people, taking refuge in a fort, were persuaded to surrender, and basely massacred. After this version of the Cawnpore tragedy on a smaller scale, the Ranee had seized the throne of her husband's ancestors, to defend it with more spirit than was shown by the would-be Peshwa.

The whole heart of the Continent remained in a state of intermittent disorder, and little could be done to put this down till the beginning of 1858, when columns of troops from Madras and Bombay respectively marched northward to clear the central districts, and rid Sir Colin Campbell of the marauding swarms that thence troubled his rear. The Bombay column, under Sir Hugh Rose, had the harder work of it. Fighting his way through a difficult country, he first relieved the English who for more than seven months had been holding out at Saugor; then moved upon Jhansi, a strongly fortified city, with a rock-built citadel towering over its walls.

The Ranee was found determined to hold out, and on March 22nd a siege of this formidable fortress had to be undertaken by two brigades of European soldiers and Sepoys. At the end of a week, they in turn became threatened by over twenty thousand rebels, under Tantia Topee, advancing to raise the siege. Fifteen hundred men, only a third of them Europeans, were all Sir Hugh Rose could spare from before the walls, but with so few he faced this fresh army, that seemed able to envelop his little band in far-stretching masses. Again, however, bold tactics were successful against a foe that seldom bore to be assailed at an unexpected point. Attacked on each flank by cavalry and artillery, the long line of Sepoys wavered, and gave way at the first onset of a handful of infantry in front. They fell back on their second line, which had no heart to renew the battle. Setting fire to the jungle in front of him, Tantia Topee fled with the loss of all his guns, hotly pursued through the blazing timber by our cavalry and artillery.

Next day but one, April 3rd, while this brilliant victory was still fresh, our soldiers carried Jhansi by assault. Severe fighting took place in the streets round the palace; then the citadel was evacuated, and the Ranee fled to Calpee, not far south of Cawnpore. Sir Hugh Rose followed, as soon as he could get supplies, defeating Tantia Topee once more on the road. Our most terrible enemy was the sun, which struck down men by hundreds; the commander himself had several sunstrokes, and more than half of one regiment fell out in a single day. Half the whole force were in the doctor's hands; hardly a man among them but was ailing. The rebels knew this weak point well, and sought to make their harassing attacks in the midday heat. The want of water also was most distressing at times; men and beasts went almost mad with thirst, when tears could be seen running from the eyes of the huge elephants sweltering on a shadeless plain, and the backs of howling dogs were burned raw by the cruel sun.

But the work seemed almost done, and in confidence of full success Sir Hugh Rose did not wait for the Madras column, which should now have joined him, but could not come up in time. At Calpee, the arsenal of the rebels, were the Ranee and Rao Sahib, a nephew of the Nana. This place also was a picturesque and imposing fortress that might well have delayed the little army. But the infatuated enemy, driven to madness by drugs and fanatical excitement, swarmed out into the labyrinth of sun-baked ravines before it, to attack our fainting soldiers; then they met with such a reception as to send them flying, not only from the field, but from the town, and their arsenal, with all its contents, fell an easy prey to the victors. This march of a thousand miles, though so briefly related, was distinguished by some of the finest feats of arms in the whole war.

The Madras column, under General Whitlock, had meanwhile had a less glorious career. After overthrowing the Nawab of Banda, it marched against the boy-Prince of Kirwi, a ward of the British Government, who was only nine years old and could hardly be accused of hostility, though his people shared the feelings of their neighbours. His palace fell without a blow. Yet its treasures were pronounced a prize of the soldiery, and the poor boy himself became dethroned for a rebellious disposition he could neither inspire nor prevent. This seems one of the most discreditable of our doings in the high-handed suppression of the Mutiny.

Leaving Whitlock's men with their easily-won booty, we return to Sir Hugh Rose, who now hoped to take well-earned repose. At the end of May he had already begun to break up his sickly force, when startling news came that the resources of the rebels were not yet exhausted. Tantia, Rao Sahib, and the Ranee had hit on the idea of seizing Gwalior, and turning it into a nucleus of renewed hostility. Scindia marched out to meet them on June 1, but a few shots decided the battle. Most of his army went over to the enemy, who seized his capital with its treasures and munitions of war, and proclaimed Nana Sahib as Peshwa. The alarming danger was that under a title once so illustrious, a revolt might still spread far southwards into the Deccan through the whole Mahratta country.

Without waiting for orders, broken in health as he was, Sir Hugh Rose lost no time in starting out to extinguish this new conflagration. By forced marches, made as far as possible at night, he reached Gwalior in a fortnight, not without encounters by the way, in one of which fell obscurely that undaunted Amazon, the young Ranee, dressed in man's clothes, whom her conqueror judged more of a man than any among the rebel leaders; the Indian Joan of Arc she has been called, and certainly makes the most heroic figure on that side of the contest. On June 19, her allies made a last useless stand before Gwalior. The pursuers followed them into the city, and next day its mighty fortress, famed as the Gibraltar of India, was audaciously broken into by a couple of subalterns, a blacksmith, and a few Sepoys. The character of the war may be seen, in which such an exploit passes with so slight notice; and these rapid successes against mighty strongholds are a remarkable contrast to the vain efforts of the mutineers to wrest from us our poor places of refuge.

Tantia Topee was followed up beyond Gwalior, and once more defeated with the loss of his guns, a matter of one charge, over in a few minutes. But that by no means made an end of this pertinacious rebel, who for the best part of a year yet was to lead our officers a weary chase all up and down the west of Central India. Through jungles and deserts, over mountains and rivers, by half-friendly, half-frightened towns, running and lurking, doubling and twisting, along a trail of some three thousand miles, he found himself everywhere hunted and headed, but could nowhere be brought effectually to bay. Here and there he might make a short stand, which always had the same result; and the nature of these encounters may be judged from one in which, with eight thousand men and thirty guns, he was routed without a single casualty on our side.

The great object was to prevent him getting south into the Deccan and stirring up the Mahrattas there to swell his shrivelled ranks, and this was successfully attained. As for catching him, that seemed more difficult. But at length he grew worn out. Such followers as were left him slunk away to their homes, or split up into wandering bands of robbers; the toils of the hunters closed round their slippery chief, fairly driven into hiding. Betrayed by a rebel who thus sought to make his peace with our Government, he was at length laid hands on in the spring of 1859, to be speedily tried and hanged, the last hydra-head of the insurrection.

For murderers like those of Cawnpore there was no pardon. But English blood ran calmer now, and wise men might talk of mercy to the misguided masses. The Governor-General had already earned the honourable nickname of "Clemency Canning," given in bitterness by those not noble enough to use victory with moderation. At the end of 1858, the Queen's proclamation offered an amnesty to all rebels who had taken no part in the murder of Europeans. This came none too soon, for the ruthless severity with which we followed our first successes had been a main cause in driving the beaten enemy to desperation, and thus prolonging a hopeless struggle.

It must be confessed with shame, that not only in the heat of combat, but in deliberate savagery excited by the licence of revenge, and with formal mockeries of justice, too many Englishmen gave themselves up to a heathen lust for bloodshed. Hasty punishment fell often on the innocent as well as the guilty, meted with the same rough measure to mutinous soldiers and to those whose crime, as in Oudh, was that of defending their country against an arrogant and powerful oppressor. The mass of the natives could hardly help themselves between one side and the other; and if they did sympathize with their own countrymen, was it for the descendants of Cromwell, of Wallace, of Alfred, to blame them so wrathfully?

Heavy could not but be the punishment that visited this unhappy land. Not a few of the mutineers were spared in battle to die by inches in some unwholesome jungle, or slunk home, when they durst, only to meet the curses of the friends upon whom they had brought so much misery, and to be at a loss how to earn their bread, pay and pension having been scattered to the winds of rebellion. The sufferings of the civil population, even where they had not risen in arms, were also pitiable; and if hundreds of homes in England had been bereaved, there would be thousands of dusky heathen to mourn their dear ones. The country was laid waste in many parts; towns and palaces were ruined; landowners were dispossessed, nobles driven into beggary among the multitude of humbler victims, whose very religion was insulted to bring home to them their defeat. A favourite mode of execution was blowing prisoners away from the mouth of guns, through which they believed themselves doomed in the shadowy life beyond death; and where they came to be hanged, the last rude offices were done by the eternally profaning touch of the sweeper caste. The temples on the river-side at Cawnpore had been blown up, as a sacrifice to the memory of our massacred country-people. The mosques and shrines of Delhi were thrown open to the infidel. Immediately after its capture, there had even been a talk of razing this great city to the ground, that its magnificence might be forgotten in its guilt.

The old king had paid dearly for that short-lived attempt to revive the glories of his ancestors. Tried by court-martial, he was transported to Rangoon, where he soon died in captivity. Certain other potentates were punished, and some rewarded at their expense, for varying conduct during a crisis when most of them had the same desire to be on the winning side, but some played their game more skilfully or more luckily than others. Nana Sahib, the most hateful of our enemies, escaped the speedy death that awaited him if ever he fell into British hands. He fled to the Himalayas with a high price on his head, and his fate was never known for certain; but the probability is that long ago he has perished more miserably than if he had been brought to the gallows.

The Power which had set up and pulled down so many princes became itself dispossessed and abolished through the upheavings of the Mutiny. In England, it was felt on all hands that such an empire as had grown out of our Eastern possessions, should no longer be left under the control of even a so dignified body as the East India Company. The realm won by private or corporate enterprise was annexed to the dominions of the British Crown; and on Nov. 1, 1858, the same proclamation which offered amnesty to the submissive rebels, declared that henceforth the Queen of England ruled as sovereign over India.

In 1877, Queen Victoria was proclaimed Empress at Delhi, amid an imposing assemblage both of actual rulers and of gorgeous native potentates bearing time-honoured titles, who thus fully acknowledged themselves vassals of the Power that in little more than a century had taken the place of the Great Mogul.

Our rule in India has now become marked by a feature almost new in the history of conquerors. We begin to recognize more and more clearly that we owe this subjugated land a debt in the elevation of her long-oppressed millions. With this duty comes a new source of danger. By the very means we take here to raise up a sense of common welfare, and through the destruction of those petty tyrannies that hitherto held apart the elements of national life, we are teaching the agglomeration of races to whom we have given a common name to look on themselves as one people, still too much differing from us in interests and sympathies; and it is to be feared that their growth in healthy progress does not keep pace with the hot-headed and loud-tongued patriotism of some who, in the schools of their rulers, have learned rather to talk about than to be fit for freedom. Though such noisy discontent is chiefly noted among the classes least formidable in arms, while the more warlike seem not unwilling to accept our supremacy, if ever another rebellion took place, we should have to deal with a less unorganized sentiment of national existence, and perhaps with the deeper and wider counsels, for want of which mainly, we have seen how the Mutiny miscarried, that else might have swept our scanty force out of India. On the other hand, in such a future emergency, we should have the advantage both of the improved scientific arms, so decisive in modern warfare, the use of which we now take more care to keep in our own hands, and of those better means of communication with the East, gained within the lifetime of our generation. In less than a month, we could throw into India as many English soldiers as, in 1857, arrived only in time to stamp out the embers of an almost ruinous conflagration.

In any case, the conscience of England has set up a new standard to judge its achievements—by the good we can do to this great people, and not by the gain we can wring from them, the honour of our mastery must stand or fall.

The work of education may well be longer and harder than that of conquest. The conduct of our countrymen here causes yet too much shame and doubt in thoughtful minds. But when we see the spirit in which many of India's rulers undertake their difficult task—the patient labours of officials, following the pattern of men like Outram, Lawrence, Havelock, the devotion to duty that often meets no reward but an early grave—we take hope that their work may after all weld into strength a free, prosperous, and united nation. And though we wisely forbear to force our faith upon these benighted souls, it rests with ourselves in time, through the power of example, to win a nobler victory than any in the blood-stained annals of Hindostan. Missionary teachings can little avail, if Christians, set among the heathen in such authority and pre-eminence, are not true to their own lessons of righteousness. Standing beside that proudly-mournful monument which now crowns the ridge of Delhi, and raises our holiest symbol over the once-rebellious city, every Englishman should be inspired to a braver struggle than with armed foes, that, mastering himself, he may rightly do his part towards planting the Cross—not in show alone, but in power—above the cruel Crescent and the hideous idols of an outworn creed!

# APPENDIX

## CHIEF DATES OF INDIAN HISTORY

| | |
|---|---|
| Alexander the Great's Invasion of India | B.C. 327 |
| Slave Kings of Delhi | A.D. 1206-90 |
| Tamerlane's Invasion | 1398 |
| Vasco de Gama's Voyage | 1498 |
| Baber founds the Mogul Empire | 1526 |
| Akbar's Reign | 1556-1605 |
| East India Company Incorporated | 1600 |
| Sivajee becomes King of the Mahrattas | 1674 |
| Death of Aurungzebe | 1707 |
| Nadir Shah plunders Delhi | 1739 |
| Clive's Defence of Arcot | 1751 |
| Battle of Plassey | 1757 |
| War with Hyder Ali | 1780 |
| Trial of Warren Hastings | 1788-95 |
| Storming of Seringapatam | 1799 |
| Battle of Assaye | 1803 |
| Overthrow of the Mahrattas | 1818 |
| First Burmese War | 1824 |
| Capture of Bhurtpore | 1827 |
| Lord William Bentinck's Governorship | 1829 |
| Disasters in Afghanistan | 1841 |
| Conquest of Scinde | 1843 |
| First Sikh War | 1845 |
| Second Sikh War | 1848 |
| Conquest of Pegu | 1852 |
| Annexation of Oudh | 1856 |
| The Sepoy Mutiny | 1857 |
| Outbreak at Meerut | May 10 |

| | |
|---|---|
| The Mutineers seize Delhi | May 11 |
| General Anson marches against Delhi | May 25 |
| Mutiny at Lucknow | May 30 |
| Mutiny at Cawnpore | June 4 |
| Mutiny at Jhansi | June 5 |
| Mutiny at Allahabad | June 6 |
| Battle of Budlee-Ka-Serai | June 8 |
| Panic Sunday at Calcutta | June 14 |
| Mutiny at Futtehgurh | June 18 |
| Massacre at Cawnpore | June 27 |
| Sir H. Lawrence defeated at Chinhut | June 30 |
| English Retreat into Agra Fort | July 5 |
| Havelock advances from Allahabad | July 7 |
| Nana Sahib routed before Cawnpore | July 16 |
| Mutiny at Dinapore | July 25 |
| Storming of Delhi | Sept. 14 |
| Surrender of the King | Sept. 21 |
| Havelock's Relief of Lucknow | Sept. 25 |
| Sir Colin Campbell marches to Lucknow | Nov. 9 |
| Residency of Lucknow evacuated | Nov. 22 |
| Tantia Topee defeated at Cawnpore | Dec. 6, 1858 |
| Lucknow finally taken | Mar. 21 |
| Taking of Jhansi | April 3 |
| Battle of Bareilly | May 5 |
| Battle before Calpee | May 22 |
| Scindia defeated by the Rebels | June 1 |
| Gwalior taken | June 19 |
| The Queen's Proclamation | Nov. 1, 1859 |
| Tantia Topee taken | April 15 |
| The Queen proclaimed Empress of India | 1877 |

**THE END.**

9 789358 007404

Printed by Libri Plureos GmbH in Hamburg, Germany